THE 48 LAWS OF

POWER

for WOMEN
fed up with
male workplace
dominance.

* The Playbook *

MARY ROBBINS

Dedication

A Special Thank You

To Selena and Brandon the source of
my motivation and Alfie (a.k.a. the furry
sock snatcher) for keeping me company
during the day!

Table of Contents

Introduction

Sarah was a brilliant and accomplished corporate professional not unlike many other women in modern workplaces. For over three decades, she worked tirelessly in challenging male-dominated industries, building a reputation as a subject matter expert in the field of engineering and security. Her personal journey was one of relentless self-improvement, technical mastery, and an unwavering commitment to her teams and employers. She always felt compelled to work harder and faster than her male counterparts to keep a seat at the table. Yet, despite her unparalleled expertise and contributions, she found herself repeatedly overlooked for promotions, underpaid for her efforts, and unrecognized in ways that mattered most.

Sarah's strengths—her technical acumen, her reliability, her team-oriented mindset—were also her greatest weaknesses. She was the first to volunteer for extra work, the first to share her expertise, and the first to prioritize her job over personal and family commitments. These qualities made her indispensable to her bosses but also made her a convenient workhorse, someone who would shoulder burdens others avoided, all while diminishing her own opportunities for advancement. She viewed collaboration and loyalty as virtues, but in the absence of strategic positioning, they left her open to exploitation by colleagues who took credit for her work and advanced their own careers at her expense.

Sarah's case is not unique. It is emblematic of the struggles faced by many women who approach their careers with a steadfast belief in hard work, collaboration, and technical excellence but who fail to recognize the game being played around them. Sarah's philosophy was rooted in the belief of meritocracy and the conviction that delivering exceptional results would naturally lead to rewards. She disdained office politics, believing they were beneath her, and trusted that her performance would speak for itself. But in corporate America, where power, influence, and perception often outweigh raw talent, this approach left her vulnerable to being exploited by those who understood the unspoken rules of the game. Sarah was me.

Throughout my career, I often felt like I was navigating a strategic game, one where the rules were unclear, yet the consequences frequently worked against me. It wasn't until I discovered Robert Greene's 48 Laws of Power that I began to understand: these were the unspoken rules being wielded against me and countless other women. Rules I was unprepared to counter or leverage to my advantage. This realization inspired me to write this book—a literal playbook designed to empower women with the same strategies men have long used to advance, achieve, and secure their power. This book is about recognizing that hard work alone is rarely enough and that navigating office dynamics requires political savviness, self-advocacy, and a clear understanding of how power flows within an organization.

This book is a guide to breaking free from the cycle of helplessness. It's a tool for women to understand that they, too, wield power and that leveraging it is not a betrayal of their values but a necessary skill for ensuring their contributions are recognized and rewarded. It is written with the hope that no woman has to sacrifice her personal life, health, or aspirations in the name of loyalty to an organization that does not reciprocate that commitment.

This book empowers readers to reclaim control over their careers. It provides strategies to navigate the complexities of workplace politics, to advocate for oneself, and to dismantle the barriers that prevent talented, hardworking women from reaching their full potential. My hope is that this book will inspire women to see their worth, claim their space, and wield their power unapologetically—not just for themselves but for the generations of women who will follow in their footsteps.

The Art of Selective Power for Women

Power isn't about doing it all—it's about doing what matters most, at the right time, in the right way. For women navigating professional and personal landscapes, this principle is even more essential. In a world where the rules of power have long been shaped by male-dominated dynamics, the ability to understand and apply power selectively can be your greatest asset.

The truth is, you don't need to master all 48 Laws of Power to be effective. Success doesn't come from trying to do everything or being everything to everyone. Instead, it comes from knowing which strategies work for you, in your unique circumstances, and applying them with confidence and precision.

Picture a woman at the top of her game. She isn't trying to outmatch everyone at everything. Instead, she's reading the room, choosing her battles, and using the tools that best suit her strengths. Whether it's guarding her reputation (Law 5), mastering timing (Law 35), or knowing when to say less (Law 4), she focuses her energy where it matters most.

The key to wielding power effectively as a woman lies in three core skills: adaptability, perception, and strategy. Adaptability means being fluid, like in Assume Formlessness (Law 48), so you can thrive in constantly shifting environments. Perception is the ability to read people and situations, drawing on laws like Discover Each Man's Thumbscrew (Law 33) to uncover motivations and leverage influence. And strategy—planning with foresight, as in Plan All the Way to the End (Law 29)—ensures that every move you make counts.

But power isn't just about using these tools; it's about defending yourself, too. In male-dominated environments, others may try to outmaneuver you with their own power plays. Recognizing tactics like Crush Your Enemy Totally (Law 15) or Play the Perfect Courtier (Law 24) allows you to protect yourself and stay one step ahead.

You don't have to be perfect or master every law to succeed. Many successful women thrive by mastering just a handful of strategies—five to ten laws applied with precision and authenticity. This isn't about changing who you are; it's about unlocking your potential to lead, influence, and rise with confidence.

This book is designed as a guide for women to navigate the complexities of power with clarity and purpose. It's not a rulebook but a toolkit—a way to adapt strategies to your unique journey. As you explore these pages, remember: the path to power is yours to define, and every choice you make is a step toward the life you want to lead.

Making the Most of This Book

Welcome to the ultimate coaching tool designed specifically for women navigating the complex dynamics of power. This book brings together all 48 Laws of Power, exploring each in ways that reflect women's unique experiences in the workplace and beyond. Every chapter dissects a law and shows you how to recognize it, leverage it to your advantage, and protect yourself when it's used against you.

The structure of this book is meant to give you flexibility. Each chapter stands alone, allowing you to choose the laws and strategies most relevant to your current challenges or goals. You don't need to read it sequentially; instead, go directly to the sections that resonate with you or match specific situations you're facing. This way, the book becomes a practical reference, a guide you can return to whenever you need insight or strategies to empower yourself.

How to Use Each Section

Each chapter is divided into several well-defined sections, each crafted to give you the tools, awareness, and strategies to navigate and master the nuances of power in a way that feels authentic and empowering.

Section 1: Understanding the Law
Each chapter begins by explaining the essence of the law. This section offers a straightforward overview, giving you a foundation for why the principle exists and how it operates in professional and social settings. It contextualizes the law in ways that help you see how it might already be showing up around you, subtly shaping interactions.

Section 2: The Power Behind the Principle
This section dives deeper into the "why" behind each law, providing insight into the psychological and social power dynamics at play. By understanding the rationale and strategy, you'll gain perspective on the potential benefits and risks. This section encourages you to think strategically, giving you the reasoning to know when and why the law is worth using to achieve specific outcomes.

Section 3: Putting It to Use

Here, you'll find actionable steps and examples on how to apply the law in a way that aligns with your goals and values. This section is filled with practical guidance to help you confidently implement each strategy, from setting professional boundaries to forming alliances with intention. By following these steps, you'll see how to leverage each principle in ways that strengthen your influence without compromising integrity.

Section 4: Recognizing When Others Use It

Power dynamics aren't one-sided, and this section helps you stay alert to signs that others might be using the law to manipulate or undermine you. This part provides you with the cues and behaviors to look for, arming you with awareness so that you can detect when someone is deploying a tactic to their advantage, potentially at your expense. Use this as a defense mechanism to avoid being blindsided.

Section 5: How to Neutralize Its Use

In this section, you'll learn specific counter-strategies to protect yourself when you sense that someone may be using a particular law against you or to advantage themselves. These suggestions give you practical ways to counter manipulative tactics and stay in control, allowing you to safeguard your boundaries and assert your position without escalating conflict. Think of this section as your personal defense toolkit.

Section 6: Behaviors that Make You a Target

Each law has associated vulnerabilities, and this section helps you identify any tendencies that could make you susceptible to exploitation. By being aware of these habits, you can actively work on behaviors that may unintentionally signal openness to manipulation. These insights allow you to reflect on your own actions and make adjustments to reinforce your resilience.

How to Get Started

To fully benefit from the strategies and insights presented, start by identifying areas where you feel most challenged or where you'd like to grow in confidence. You may find it helpful to take notes on how each law applies to your experiences and what adjustments or actions you might take. Use the "Putting It to Use" steps to outline practical changes, and review "How to Neutralize Its Use" to strengthen your defenses and mitigate attacks.

The book also encourages a level of self-reflection and growth. Many of the "Behaviors that Make You a Target" sections invite you to look inward, considering your tendencies and examining if any habits are unintentionally working against you. This awareness is one of the most empowering tools you can cultivate, as it enables you to make conscious choices that protect your agency and integrity.

Ultimately, this book is designed as a guide, offering you not just information but also the confidence to understand, navigate, and master the dynamics of power in a way that respects your values and amplifies your influence. Use it whenever you need perspective, reinforcement, or a fresh strategy. And remember, each chapter is a resource—return to specific laws as your circumstances shift, and adapt the principles as you evolve on your journey.

Authors Note:
The titles of the laws are Robert Greene's, drawn from his study of how power was wielded by rulers, emperors, and political figures throughout history. While some sound controversial or dramatic, they reflect his effort to capture the nature of power in those past contexts. This book is an independent work of interpretation, referencing those titles as a foundation for translation, reframing, and reimagining them for women in today's workplace—offered not for manipulation, but as tools for awareness, protection, and empowerment.

PART I

Laying the Foundation for Power

Law 1: Never Outshine the Master
Protect your growth by allowing others to feel secure in their authority.

Law 2: Never Put Too Much Trust in Friends, Learn How to Use Enemies
Build strategic alliances that serve your goals.

Law 3: Conceal Your Intentions
Keep your plans private until you're ready to act.

Law 4: Always Say Less Than Necessary
Learn the power of silence and control the narrative.

Law 5: So Much Depends on Reputation —Guard it with Your Life
Your reputation is your most valuable asset—protect it fiercely.

Law— **1**

Never Outshine the Master

"True strength lies in lifting others up without dimming your own light."

— Unknown

Law 1: Never Outshine the Master

This law advises that you should never outshine or appear more competent than those in positions of power above you. By making superiors feel secure and in control, you avoid their insecurity, which might lead to their attempt to undermine you.

The Power Behind the Principle

People in power are often insecure and may perceive others who surpass them in skill or competence as a threat. By being modest and letting them take credit for achievements, you secure their favor and avoid unnecessary conflict. The benefit is maintaining harmony with those in authority and gaining their trust.

Putting It to Use (if you are the subordinate)

- Acknowledge their superiority and show deference, even if subtly.
- Avoid direct competition with them in any area they dominate.
- Make them feel that you are not a threat by focusing on their strengths.
- Offer public praise for their ideas or decisions.
- Stay out of the spotlight when it would make them feel insecure.
- Focus on personal growth in areas where they are not focused.
- Never undermine their position or attempt to outperform them in their area.
- Offer solutions to problems that don't threaten their authority.
- Be cautious about expressing opinions that could challenge their decisions.
- Build their trust by being a dependable, quiet support rather than a rival.

Recognizing When Others Try to Diminish Your Role

- They praise you excessively to make you feel safe and appreciated.
- They downplay their own achievements or exaggerate yours in front of others.
- They subtly attempt to keep you in the background.
- They ignore or dismiss your contributions when speaking about team success.
- They give you more responsibility without recognition.
- They downplay your expertise in front of others.

- They create situations where you are forced to defer to them.
- They constantly seek to remind you of their superior experience or position.
- They maintain a façade of benevolence while subtly controlling or manipulating your moves.
- They feed you just enough praise to maintain your loyalty without truly elevating you.

How to Neutralize the Opportunist (if you're the boss)

- **Establish Clear Boundaries:** Set clear expectations regarding roles and responsibilities to reinforce authority and prevent attempts to overstep.
- **Encourage Team-Based Recognition:** Emphasize team accomplishments rather than individual praise, reducing the likelihood of someone standing out excessively.
- **Acknowledge Their Contributions Publicly:** Control the narrative by openly acknowledging their efforts yourself, framing their accomplishments as part of your mentorship or leadership.
- **Delegate Strategically:** Assign tasks that showcase their strengths without overshadowing your authority, keeping their role defined within your vision.
- **Solicit Regular Feedback:** Frequently ask for input from all team members to dilute the influence of any one individual and reinforce a collaborative culture.
- **Promote Cross-Training:** Encourage other team members to learn the skills of the ambitious individual, spreading their unique knowledge across the team to balance influence.
- **Provide Constructive Criticism:** Offer feedback that helps them improve while reminding them of areas where they still need guidance or growth, subtly reaffirming your position as their leader.
- **Build Alliances with Key Team Members:** Cultivate strong relationships with other team members, ensuring that loyalty and support are not overly concentrated on any one person.
- **Publicly Support the Chain of Command:** Reinforce the importance of hierarchy and structure within the organization, making it clear that everyone is accountable to a larger framework.
- **Assign Complex, High-Level Projects:** Take on challenging projects or strategic initiatives that highlight your unique skills and vision, reaffirming your expertise and authority in areas they cannot replicate.

Behaviors that Make You a Target

There are certain behaviors that can signal to someone to deploy manipulation tactics to gain favor or advantage. Here are some behaviors that can make you more susceptible to this kind of influence:

- **Seeking Constant Validation**: If a superior frequently seeks reassurance or praise, it signals a need for validation, making them more receptive to flattery and deference from subordinates.
- **Showing Insecurity or Self-Doubt**: A superior who openly displays insecurity, self-doubt, or lack of confidence might be more likely to respond positively to a subordinate who avoids outshining them and plays up the superior's strengths.
- **Overemphasis on Hierarchy and Authority**: A superior who constantly reinforces their position or authority may be signaling that they feel the need to assert control, making them more susceptible to subordinates who skillfully flatter and defer to that authority.
- **Being Overly Competitive**: A superior who frequently compares themselves to others or shows jealousy over others' achievements might be especially influenced by a subordinate who tactfully avoids outshining them and highlights the superior's accomplishments instead.
- **Craving Loyalty and Allegiance**: If a superior highly values loyalty and places significant emphasis on „team unity" or personal allegiance, a subordinate can manipulate them by acting as a loyal supporter, reinforcing the superior's ego and sense of authority.
- **Micromanaging Tasks and Projects**: A superior who micromanages or struggles to delegate may indicate they need to feel indispensable. This invites subordinates to appear dependent on the superior's guidance, subtly reinforcing their sense of control.
- **Inconsistent Recognition of Contributions**: If a superior is inconsistent in recognizing or valuing the team's contributions, it can indicate uncertainty or favoritism. Subordinates might exploit this by downplaying their achievements, making the superior feel more secure and in control.
- **Displaying a Need for Personal Attention**: Superiors who are visibly uncomfortable when attention shifts away from them or who seek to be the focus of meetings or discussions may be more vulnerable to subordinates

who avoid taking the spotlight and constantly reinforce the superior's centrality.

- **Demonstrating Emotional Reactivity to Praise and Criticism**: If a superior reacts strongly—positively to praise and negatively to criticism—it signals that they may be swayed by subordinates who tactfully cater to their emotional responses with strategic praise.
- **Being Overly Trusting of Flattery**: A superior who is highly responsive to compliments or flattery may not recognize when a subordinate is manipulating them, making it easier for the subordinate to control the superior's perceptions and responses by appealing to their ego.

Law —— **2**

Never Put Too Much Trust in Friends, Learn How to Use Enemies

---

"Keep your friends close, and your enemies closer."

— *Sun Tzu*

Law 2: Never Put Too Much Trust in Friends, Learn How to Use Enemies

This law suggests being cautious with friends in positions of trust, as they may betray you out of envy or entitlement. Instead, you can gain power by strategically managing relationships with those who may not be close allies, as they often respect professional boundaries.

The Power Behind the Principle

Friends can become complacent, expecting leniency and, at times, acting out of jealousy. Enemies, however, are likely to remain alert, cautious, and grateful for opportunities, making them more predictable and manageable. The benefit is reduced betrayal risk and the ability to leverage multiple perspectives and motivations.

Putting It to Use

- **Build Relationships with Former Rivals**: Reach out to former competitors or adversaries, showing genuine interest in finding common ground to turn past conflict into mutual benefit.
- **Remain Objective and Cautious with Friends**: Avoid blindly trusting friends in business or strategic matters; ensure agreements and responsibilities are clear to prevent misunderstandings or disappointments.
- **Leverage Enemies' Motivation**: Recognize that enemies often have a strong incentive to prove their worth or redeem themselves, which can make them surprisingly loyal and committed partners.
- **Use Friends for Support, Not Dependence**: Rely on friends for moral support or camaraderie, but avoid making them solely responsible for critical tasks to reduce the risk of complacency or taking advantage of your trust.
- **Identify Shared Goals with Rivals**: Find specific goals or objectives that you and a former rival both stand to benefit from, establishing a foundation for a collaborative partnership.
- **Engage in Strategic Compromises**: Make small, calculated compromises with an enemy to demonstrate your willingness to cooperate, which can encourage reciprocal actions and build trust.

- **Maintain Professional Boundaries with Friends**: Keep a professional distance and establish boundaries, ensuring personal relationships don't interfere with objective decision-making.
- **Turn Enemies into Allies Through Acknowledgment**: Show respect for an enemy's strengths and accomplishments, subtly positioning yourself as someone who values their contributions, which can open the door to alliance.
- **Focus on Mutual Benefits**: Highlight the practical benefits of working with a former enemy, emphasizing how collaboration could bring rewards that neither party could achieve alone.
- **Avoid Relying Solely on Loyalty**: Recognize that loyalty can be fragile; base your trust on competence and mutual interests rather than friendship or loyalty alone.

Recognizing When Others Use It

- They avoid sharing too much personal information.
- They quickly forgive former rivals and show trust in new alliances.
- They praise former enemies to gain their support.
- They maintain a professional but distant relationship with friends.
- They offer significant responsibilities to people they barely know.
- They express skepticism about traditional friendships in business.
- They avoid confiding in longtime friends on major projects.
- They evaluate people's utility over loyalty.
- They openly prefer neutrality to close alliances.
- They distance themselves when friends seek favors or support.

How to Neutralize Its Use

- Maintain a professional boundary, even with close friends.
- Be cautious when sharing sensitive information, especially if others are aware.
- Refrain from feeling entitled to special treatment due to a friendship.
- Focus on your value and contributions rather than on loyalty expectations.
- Build a network that includes professional contacts, not just friends.
- Avoid favoritism in your relationships at work.
- Be prepared for constructive criticism from all relationships.
- Keep your personal motivations clear and separate from work matters.
- Embrace a balanced, neutral approach to professional friendships.

- Avoid depending on friendships alone to move forward; let your work speak.

Behaviors that Make You a Target

- **Blindly Trusting Friends**: Showing unquestioning faith in friends or close colleagues may signal that you're overly reliant on loyalty, making it easy for others to take advantage of your trust.
- **Over-sharing Personal Information**: Sharing too many personal details or insecurities with friends in professional contexts can make you vulnerable to manipulation, as they may use this information to influence your decisions.
- **Avoiding Constructive Criticism**: Hesitating to question or critique friends' actions might make you seem overly deferential, encouraging them to take liberties or cut corners with your approval.
- **Relying on Friends for Key Tasks or Decisions**: Depending solely on friends to handle critical responsibilities may suggest that you lack objectivity, allowing them to shape outcomes without oversight.
- **Ignoring Red Flags**: Overlooking signs of unreliability or incompetence in friends signals that you may tolerate poor performance or excuses, opening the door for exploitation.
- **Distancing Yourself from Former Rivals**: Refusing to consider alliances with past adversaries can make you appear inflexible or overly loyal, which friends might exploit, knowing you're unlikely to seek alternative support.
- **Focusing on Personal Loyalty Over Competence**: Valuing loyalty more than ability might indicate you're willing to overlook faults, encouraging friends to manipulate situations to their advantage.
- **Showing Emotional Attachment in Decision-Making**: Allowing emotions to guide your professional relationships may make you appear easily influenced, prompting others to exploit your emotions to gain control.
- **Refusing to Collaborate with "Enemies"**: Demonstrating a reluctance to work with former rivals or competitors may suggest to friends that they have an exclusive hold on your trust, potentially leading them to misuse it.
- **Confusing Personal and Professional Boundaries**: Blurring the line between friendship and professionalism can invite manipulation, as friends may feel entitled to favors or special treatment, using personal ties to sway your decisions.

Law— **3**

Conceal Your Intentions

"He who does not reveal his intentions has already won half of the game."

— *Baltasar Gracián*

Law 3: Conceal Your Intentions

This law encourages maintaining an air of mystery by hiding your true motives, ensuring that others cannot anticipate your plans or actions. Concealing intentions allows you to work strategically and avoid premature resistance.

The Power Behind the Principle

When people know your intentions, they can prepare defenses, manipulate, or obstruct your plans. Concealing intentions keeps others guessing, which can lead to underestimations or misinterpretations in your favor. The benefit is gaining the advantage of surprise and controlling the narrative around your actions.

Putting It to Use

- **Use Ambiguity in Communication**: When discussing plans, speak in general terms rather than revealing specific goals or intentions, creating an air of mystery around your true motives.
- **Reveal Red Herrings**: Occasionally share minor, unrelated details or "fake" objectives that distract others from your real goals, keeping them focused on the wrong thing.
- **Control the Flow of Information**: Limit who has access to complete information about your plans by sharing only selective details with different people, preventing any single individual from seeing the full picture.
- **Mirror Others' Language and Ideas**: By mirroring the ideas or language of those around you, you can seem aligned with their goals, which helps conceal your own intentions and blend in.
- **Practice Strategic Vagueness**: When asked about your intentions, respond with vague answers or shift focus to long-term goals, sidestepping any concrete revelations.
- **Ask Leading Questions Instead of Making Statements**: Direct attention away from your own intentions by asking questions about others' views, subtly encouraging them to share more without revealing your position.
- **Use Decoy Plans**: Set up an obvious plan or project that diverts attention from your actual intentions. Others may focus on the decoy, leaving your true objectives hidden.

- **Project Disinterest**: Appear indifferent or less invested in areas where you have strong intentions, which makes your true goals less obvious and keeps people from probing further.
- **Adopt a Routine to Avoid Attention**: Maintain a predictable or routine approach in public, while making moves toward your goals in private, reducing the chances that others will notice changes or hidden plans.
- **Provide Partial Transparency**: Share just enough information to appear open and trustworthy, but keep critical details to yourself. This will satisfy others' curiosity without revealing your full intentions.

Recognizing When Others Use It

- They frequently change topics or avoid direct answers.
- They use vague language or generalities rather than specifics.
- They avoid making commitments or clear statements.
- They offer minimal detail about their goals or plans.
- They deflect questions with humor or flattery.
- They act unpredictably or contradict their previous actions.
- They appear to agree but avoid committing resources.
- They remain noncommittal in group decisions.
- They redirect focus toward other unrelated subjects.
- They speak about possibilities rather than specific outcomes.

How to Neutralize Its Use

- Ask direct, open-ended questions to gauge their intentions.
- Rephrase their statements to clarify understanding.
- Observe their actions over time rather than focusing solely on words.
- Seek out corroborating information from other sources.
- Maintain a neutral stance until you understand their goals.
- Encourage collaboration that requires them to reveal some intentions.
- Document agreements and decisions to clarify vague statements.
- Remain calm and patient rather than pressing them for answers.
- Verify details with others who may also be affected.
- Stay observant and assess their patterns of behavior.

Behaviors that Make You a Target

- **Oversharing Plans and Goals**: Frequently sharing your intentions, even in casual conversations, signals openness and transparency, making it easier for others to anticipate and potentially manipulate your moves.
- **Being Predictable**: Acting in a routine, consistent way without variation can signal that your actions are easy to foresee, allowing others to plan around your patterns to influence outcomes.
- **Expressing Goals or Desires Too Early**: Revealing what you want or hope to achieve at the start of a project or negotiation gives others the upper hand, as they can adjust their actions to exploit your goals.
- **Showing Emotional Reactions**: Displaying strong emotional responses can reveal what matters most to you, making it easier for others to manipulate you by using those triggers.
- **Taking Everyone's Advice at Face Value**: Acting on others' advice without critical assessment signals trustfulness, allowing others to subtly steer your decisions by framing their advice to their advantage.
- **Trusting Easily and Quickly**: Quickly building trust with others without verification or restraint can make you appear naïve, inviting others to manipulate your intentions by pretending to be supportive.
- **Revealing Frustrations or Weaknesses**: Openly discussing frustrations or challenges can signal where you may lack control, encouraging others to use this information to redirect or block your efforts.
- **Avoiding Strategic Silence**: Speaking up constantly without employing pauses or silence can signal impulsiveness, allowing others to manipulate situations by patiently waiting for you to reveal your intentions.
- **Sharing Every Step of Your Process**: Describing the details of your strategies and decision-making process signals full transparency, making it easier for others to anticipate your next moves.
- **Assuming Everyone Has Positive Intentions**: Expecting that others have no hidden agendas might signal innocence or lack of experience, making it easier for people to deceive or influence you by hiding their true motives.

*Law—*4

Always Say Less Than Necessary

"A wise woman speaks only what's essential, leaving room for her silence to be heard."

— Unknown

Law 4: Always Say Less Than Necessary

This law encourages limiting the amount of information you reveal. By speaking less, you gain more control over what others know, creating an air of mystery and leaving them curious or even intimidated.

The Power Behind the Principle

When you talk too much, you are more likely to reveal unnecessary information, which others could use to their advantage. Speaking less keeps you in control and gives others fewer opportunities to analyze or misinterpret your intentions. The benefit is that others may project their own assumptions onto you, often leading them to underestimate or respect you more.

Putting It to Use

- **Use Concise Language**: Practice getting to the point quickly without unnecessary elaboration. Say only what's needed to convey your message clearly and stop before over-explaining.
- **Pause Before Responding**: Take a brief pause before answering questions or joining discussions. This pause creates an impression of thoughtfulness and prevents impulsive, excessive speech.
- **Let Others Fill the Silence**: Embrace moments of silence during conversations, allowing the other person to speak more. This encourages them to reveal information while you maintain a mysterious, controlled presence.
- **Answer Questions Selectively**: When asked questions, respond only to the parts you find necessary. Avoid volunteering additional details unless specifically asked, keeping your intentions and knowledge more concealed.
- **Use Open-Ended Statements**: Make statements that imply a broader meaning without spelling it out entirely. This encourages others to interpret your words in ways that suit their assumptions, maintaining ambiguity.
- **Choose Neutral Language**: Use language that's vague or neutral rather than definitive or detailed. This leaves room for interpretation and minimizes the risk of overcommitment or exposure.

- **Listen More Than You Speak**: Actively listen to others and give minimal responses. Acknowledge their points without adding your own perspective unnecessarily, allowing you to gather insights without revealing much.
- **Avoid Personal Revelations**: In both professional and social settings, refrain from discussing personal details, preferences, or intentions. This maintains your privacy and prevents others from using your information.
- **Practice Ending Conversations Gracefully**: Learn to end conversations at a natural stopping point rather than elaborating or circling back. A simple "That's all I wanted to mention" or "I believe that covers it" can conclude discussions cleanly.
- **Use Noncommittal Responses**: Respond to questions with phrases like "That's interesting" or "We'll see," without committing to any specific stance. This preserves your flexibility and leaves others guessing about your true thoughts.

Recognizing When Others Use It

- They frequently respond with short, ambiguous answers.
- They avoid offering opinions unless directly asked.
- They often nod or acknowledge without elaborating.
- They ask questions rather than providing information.
- They pause before answering, making their responses feel measured.
- They steer conversations back to you or other people.
- They seem guarded or unemotional when discussing plans.
- They rarely share personal stories or insights.
- They seem comfortable with silence in discussions.
- They use statements that leave room for interpretation.

How to Neutralize Its Use

- Prompt users with open-ended questions that require elaboration.
- Share enough of your own perspective to encourage reciprocation.
- Observe nonverbal cues for additional insight.
- Stay attentive to any contradictions or inconsistencies over time.
- Politely ask for clarification when responses are vague.
- Avoid filling silences and let them reveal more if they choose.
- Engage them in collaborative tasks that encourage openness.

- Paraphrase their responses to confirm understanding.
- Revisit points they've been brief on to gather more.
- Maintain your composure, not showing discomfort with their reserve.

Behaviors that Make You a Target

- **Over-explaining or Justifying Actions**: Constantly explaining yourself or justifying your decisions can signal insecurity or a need for validation, making it easier for others to manipulate you by questioning or probing further.
- **Revealing Personal Details Freely**: Sharing too much about your personal life or emotions can make you vulnerable, as others may use this information to influence or sway your decisions.
- **Filling Silences Out of Nervousness**: Feeling uncomfortable with silence and filling it with unnecessary information can reveal more than intended, inviting others to guide conversations to extract insights.
- **Seeking Approval Through Talking**: Trying to gain approval or acceptance by over-sharing can make you appear eager to please, allowing others to manipulate you by withholding validation until you reveal more.
- **Being Impulsive in Conversations**: Speaking without pausing or considering your words may signal impulsiveness, making it easy for others to steer conversations and lead you to disclose more than planned.
- **Giving Detailed Explanations for Simple Points**: Providing excessive detail when it's not required can indicate a lack of confidence or desire to be understood, which can prompt others to pressure you for even more information.
- **Volunteering Sensitive Information**: Offering sensitive or confidential details unprompted can make you an easy target, as others realize they can extract information without much effort.
- **Using Emotional Language**: Speaking with high emotional intensity can reveal personal attachments or biases, encouraging others to manipulate you by tapping into those emotions.
- **Agreeing to Clarify on Demand**: Being quick to clarify or expand on every point can show that you are open to sharing everything, making it easy for others to keep probing for more details.
- **Talking More Than Listening**: Dominating conversations instead of listening can signal that you're likely to reveal too much, making it easy for others to manipulate by allowing you to talk freely while they gather information.

Law— **5**

So Much Depends on Reputation – Guard it with Your Life

"Your reputation is your armor; protect it as fiercely as you protect your dreams."

— K. Bailes

Law 5: So Much Depends on Reputation – Guard it with Your Life

This law emphasizes the importance of reputation as a powerful asset. Protecting your reputation keeps you respected and trustworthy, while even a small blemish can lead others to doubt your value and reliability.

The Power Behind the Principle

A solid reputation is a source of influence and respect, often preceding your actions. By diligently protecting your reputation, you minimize risks of slander and rumors that can harm your standing. The benefit is maintaining credibility, influence, and opportunities, as well as deterring rivals from attempting to undermine you.

Putting It to Use

- **Be Consistent in Actions and Words**: Ensure that your behavior aligns with the image you wish to project. Any discrepancy can damage your reputation. Consistency breeds trust and respect.
- **Master the Art of Strategic Silence**: Sometimes saying nothing is more powerful than engaging in unnecessary conversations. Know when to stay silent to avoid saying something that could be used against you.
- **Control the Narrative**: Actively manage how others perceive you by carefully crafting the story of your life. This can be done by cultivating a strong presence in social settings, sharing your achievements, and framing your contributions positively.
- **Monitor Your Associations**: Who you surround yourself with directly affects your reputation. Avoid associating with people who might harm your image or reputation.
- **Handle Criticism with Grace**: Don't respond impulsively to criticism. Instead, address it thoughtfully or use it as an opportunity to enhance your standing, showing you are both humble and strong.
- **Project Confidence, Not Arrogance**: Confidence attracts respect, while arrogance invites hostility. Develop an aura of assuredness without appearing condescending.

- **Anticipate and Deflect Attacks**: Be aware of potential threats to your reputation, whether through gossip, sabotage, or attacks. Deflect or neutralize them swiftly by preemptively addressing any rumors or falsehoods.
- **Be Aware of Your Public Image**: Monitor how you are perceived in public spaces. Whether it's your online presence, personal interactions, or professional conduct, make sure your image reflects the kind of reputation you want.
- **Don't Over-Extend Yourself**: Saying yes to everything can make you seem unreliable. Protect your reputation by being selective with your commitments, ensuring you only promise what you can deliver.
- **Use Social Proof and Testimonials**: Leverage positive testimonials and endorsements to reinforce your reputation. Having others speak highly of you, especially those who are respected, can enhance your credibility.

Recognizing When Others Use It

- They are meticulous about image and presentation in public settings.
- They quickly address or clarify any rumors involving them.
- They actively manage their social media presence and professional image.
- They frequently talk about their accomplishments or successes.
- They avoid associating with people who might damage their reputation.
- They redirect conversations to focus on their reliability or trustworthiness.
- They counter negative remarks about themselves with subtle corrections.
- They show defensiveness when their past actions are questioned.
- They monitor others' opinions and feedback closely.
- They align themselves with individuals of high standing to boost their image.

How to Neutralize Its Use

- Build a credible reputation of your own to prevent dependency on others' views.
- Document and share your achievements to reinforce your standing.
- Address any misunderstandings or false information directly.
- Stay consistent in your actions and commitments to build trust.
- Avoid engaging in gossip or situations that could harm your reputation.
- Build alliances with those who share or support your values.
- Be cautious when associating with individuals whose values differ from yours.

- Regularly review your social media and online presence.
- Display confidence in your actions without appearing defensive.
- Approach conflicts calmly, focusing on resolution rather than rebuttal.

Behaviors that Make You a Target

- **Over-Sharing Personal Information**: Revealing too much about your personal life can make you vulnerable to manipulation. Others can use your weaknesses against you if they know your insecurities or sensitive areas.
- **Being Too Eager to Please**: Constantly seeking approval or trying to please others can make you seem desperate for validation, making you an easy target for manipulation as others may exploit your desire for acceptance.
- **Ignoring the Importance of First Impressions**: Dismissing the power of reputation in the early stages of a relationship or interaction can lead to long-term damage. If you don't guard your reputation from the start, it may be too late to fix it later.
- **Allowing Your Emotions to Drive Decisions**: If you act impulsively or let emotions guide your actions, people may view you as unstable or easy to manipulate. This could cause a tarnishing of your reputation.
- **Being Inconsistent**: If your words and actions don't align, or you are erratic in your behavior, it will confuse others and lower your standing. Inconsistency makes you appear unreliable, and people will be more willing to exploit you.
- **Exposing Your Vulnerabilities**: While it's important to be human, revealing too much vulnerability can invite exploitation. If you reveal your fears or weaknesses to the wrong people, they may use that against you to manipulate your decisions.
- **Being a Doormat**: Letting others take advantage of you without setting boundaries invites manipulation. If people perceive that you'll always give in to pressure, they will feel free to manipulate you for their benefit.
- **Engaging in Gossip**: Spreading gossip or listening to others gossip can damage your reputation. Gossip can quickly become a tool used against you, as others may turn the conversation back on you or use what you've shared to undermine you.
- **Letting Others Control the Narrative About You**: If you don't actively protect your reputation and let others dictate how they view you, you risk being manipulated into a narrative that harms your status and power.

- **Being Overly Trusting**: Blindly trusting others without considering their motives can lead to betrayal and manipulation. If you're too trusting, people may take advantage of your good nature to advance their own agendas at your expense.

PART II

Owning Your Influence

Law 6: Court Attention at All Costs
Stand out for the right reasons and make your presence known.

Law 7: Get Others to Do the Work for You, but Always Take the Credit
Delegate effectively and claim your accomplishments.

Law 8: Make Others Come to You—Use Bait if Necessary
Draw people to your terms without chasing after them.

Law 9: Win Through Your Actions, Not Arguments
Let your results speak louder than words

Law 10: Infection: Avoid the Unhappy and Unlucky
Surround yourself with people who elevate your energy and potential.

Law— **6**

Court Attention at All Costs

"There's only one thing in life worse than being talked about, and that is not being talked about."

— Oscar Wilde

Law 6: Court Attention at All Costs

This law advises that attracting attention is essential for standing out and gaining influence. Whether through positive or controversial means, keeping attention focused on you amplifies your presence and power.

The Power Behind the Principle

People often ignore what they do not notice, and invisibility can render you powerless. By actively courting attention, you remain relevant, allowing you to control the narrative around your actions and intentions. The benefit is increased influence, visibility, and the potential to shape others' perceptions of you.

Putting It to Use

- **Be Unpredictable**: Keep people guessing about what you'll do next. By being unpredictable, you draw attention to yourself because people are intrigued by the unexpected. Think of it like a show where the audience is eager to see what happens next.
- **Master the Art of Drama**: Drama captures people's attention. If you find ways to add a little intrigue or spectacle to your life or business, people will naturally gravitate toward you. This doesn't mean unnecessary chaos, but creating a memorable, captivating presence.
- **Create a Unique Identity**: Develop a persona or style that stands out. Whether it's your clothing, your speech, or your mannerisms, make sure there's something distinctive about you that makes people take notice.
- **Use the Power of Mystery**: Keep some aspects of your life and personality veiled in mystery. When people can't figure you out completely, they'll keep paying attention, trying to understand you. It's human nature to be intrigued by mystery.
- **Generate Controversy (Carefully)**: Controversy often puts you at the center of attention. However, use it strategically. Say or do something bold that challenges the status quo or sparks debate, but ensure it doesn't backfire or damage your reputation permanently.
- **Network with High-Profile Individuals**: Associating with influential or high-status individuals automatically elevates your profile. People will pay

attention to you because of who you're seen with, so carefully curate your social and professional connections.

- **Create a Signature Move or Quote**: Develop something that people can easily associate with you—a catchphrase, a signature gesture, or a memorable accomplishment. This will ensure you stand out in people's minds and remain at the forefront of their attention.
- **Be the Center of Conversation**: Whether at a party, a meeting, or on social media, make sure you contribute in a way that places you at the center of attention. This can be done through humor, provocative ideas, or simply being the most engaging person in the room.
- **Make Your Presence Known in Key Situations**: Identify moments where you can enter the spotlight, whether it's a business meeting, a social gathering, or a public event. At those times, make your presence known and be the person who people remember afterward.
- **Leverage Social Media and Publicity**: In the modern age, social media is a powerful tool to court attention. Consistently engage with your audience, share unique content, and create a strong digital persona that attracts attention and followers.

Recognizing When Others Use It

- They frequently engage in dramatic or bold actions.
- They dress or speak in a way that draws immediate attention.
- They share accomplishments publicly, even minor ones.
- They use controversy or shock tactics to stay relevant.
- They often interrupt conversations to redirect focus to themselves.
- They make grand, exaggerated statements about their goals.
- They are quick to engage in debates or discussions, even on trivial issues.
- They involve themselves in various high-profile or visible projects.
- They mention influential connections or notable accomplishments.
- They use social media heavily to project their presence.

How to Neutralize Its Use

- Set clear boundaries to limit distractions from their behavior.
- Focus on substance over flair in your own interactions.
- Counter with facts or data if their statements are exaggerated.

- Maintain a calm demeanor to avoid getting drawn into their theatrics.
- Steer conversations toward constructive, team-focused outcomes.
- Avoid excessive engagement in their attention-seeking behavior.
- Shift focus back to shared goals or tasks during discussions.
- Recognize and appreciate their skills without enabling constant attention.
- Encourage balanced representation in collaborative settings.
- Focus on quality work and reliability to build your own standing.

Behaviors that Make You a Target

- **Being Too Shy or Invisible**: If you deliberately keep a low profile and avoid the spotlight, others may take advantage of your obscurity. People who are invisible can easily be ignored or sidelined, making them susceptible to manipulation.
- **Over-Compensating for Attention**: Desperately seeking attention in ways that come across as needy or fake (e.g., seeking validation at all costs) makes you appear weak and insecure. Others will use this to manipulate or control you.
- **Failing to Stand Out**: Blending in too much with the crowd makes it difficult for you to be noticed or valued. If you don't make an effort to distinguish yourself, others can easily overlook or dismiss you, which puts you in a vulnerable position to be manipulated.
- **Being Predictable and Boring**: If you're too predictable or lack excitement in your actions and ideas, people will stop paying attention to you. Once attention fades, you become easier to manipulate because you lack the visibility and influence to resist manipulation.
- **Over-Explaining Yourself**: If you're constantly seeking to explain or justify your actions in a way that diminishes your mystique, you make yourself easier to control. People lose interest when they feel they can predict your every move or thought.
- **Being Overly Humble**: Extreme humility that leads to underplaying your accomplishments or talents can cause you to fade into the background. When you downplay your abilities, people are less likely to notice you, and others might take credit for your achievements.
- **Letting Others Steal the Spotlight**: Constantly letting others take the lead or hog attention can put you in a position where you're ignored. While being

supportive is valuable, giving others all the focus leaves you vulnerable to manipulation and sidelining.

- **Focusing Solely on Practicality**: If you only focus on practicality and avoid showing any flair or creativity, people will stop paying attention to you. You need to provide more than just utility; people are attracted to those who bring something unique and engaging to the table.
- **Avoiding Conflict at All Costs**: Never rocking the boat or avoiding necessary conflict can make you appear passive and non-confrontational. This puts you in a weak position where you're more likely to be taken advantage of by more dominant personalities.
- **Constantly Seeking Validation from Others**: If you're always seeking praise or approval, you give others the power to control how you feel about yourself. This makes you an easy target for manipulation because your sense of worth is tied to external validation rather than your own sense of self.

Law— **7**

Get Others to Do the Work for You, but Always Take the Credit

---

"Empower others to help you rise, but honor your contribution boldly."

— Unknown

Law 7: Get Others to Do the Work for You, but Always Take the Credit

This law suggests leveraging the efforts and talents of others to achieve your goals while taking responsibility for the success. By delegating tasks while maintaining a central role, you conserve energy and resources while amplifying your accomplishments.

The Power Behind the Principle

Enlisting others to contribute allows you to accomplish more without depleting your own time and effort. Taking credit not only reinforces your leadership but also positions you as the driving force behind successes. The benefit is enhanced productivity and influence with minimal personal expenditure.

Putting It to Use

- **Delegate Tasks Strategically**: Identify the skills of those around you and delegate tasks accordingly. Use the strengths of others to accomplish your goals more efficiently, but make sure you oversee the outcome and maintain control of the narrative.
- **Be the Visionary**: Position yourself as the person with the grand vision, while letting others handle the specifics and execution. By maintaining the vision, you ensure that all credit for the final product or outcome is attributed to you.
- **Use Subordinates as Extensions of Your Will**: Frame your team or colleagues as extensions of your strategic mind. Let them do the work, but ensure they know that they are working toward your ultimate goal, with you at the helm.
- **Cultivate a Reputation for Leadership**: Build your image as a strong leader who brings out the best in others. When things go well, you take the credit for orchestrating the success; when things go wrong, you can deflect blame to the executioners.
- **Take Credit for Team Achievements**: When a group project or collaborative effort succeeds, make sure to highlight your role in coordinating or guiding the effort. Even if the actual work was done by others, position yourself as the mastermind who pulled everything together.

- **Use Others' Ideas as Your Own**: If someone presents a good idea, don't hesitate to adopt it as your own. Give credit where it's due when necessary, but take the lead in implementing it and make sure the recognition goes to you.
- **Provide Direction, Not Labor**: While others are performing the actual work, focus on providing high-level guidance, direction, and motivation. Your input should be strategic, while their labor handles the practical aspects of implementation.
- **Highlight Your Influence in Success**: In any success, whether personal or professional, make sure to highlight how your influence, leadership, or expertise contributed to the outcome. This reinforces the narrative that you were key to the success, even if you weren't the one doing the bulk of the work.
- **Take the Lead in Problem-Solving**: If an issue arises, position yourself as the one who solves the problem, even if the solution was conceived by someone else. By stepping in at critical moments, you reinforce your role as the ultimate decision-maker.
- **Reward Publicly, Control Privately**: While you delegate the work, make sure to publicly praise those who contributed. This can foster loyalty and make people eager to help in the future, while still ensuring that you are the one who receives the lion's share of the credit and recognition.

Recognizing When Others Use It

- They frequently delegate tasks without clear reasons.
- They highlight results without mentioning team members involved.
- They take credit in group settings without acknowledging others.
- They emphasize their role even in tasks where they were minimally involved.
- They quickly adopt successful ideas from others as their own.
- They are absent during challenging times but present for accomplishments.
- They praise others' work privately but not publicly.
- They subtly downplay others' contributions when discussing outcomes.
- They strategically align themselves with talented individuals.
- They deflect questions on specifics, focusing on overall success.

How to Neutralize Its Use

- Document your contributions and share them with relevant parties.
- Politely assert your role in group settings to clarify your input.
- Seek recognition from trusted team members or leaders.
- Encourage a collaborative credit system for group achievements.
- Set clear boundaries regarding shared tasks and responsibilities.
- Advocate for equitable acknowledgment of each team member's role.
- Focus on building your reputation for specific, impactful contributions.
- Be prepared to present your work when the opportunity arises.
- Foster relationships with individuals who value transparency.
- Avoid confrontation by focusing on subtle reinforcement of your work.

Behaviors that Make You a Target

- **Doing Everything Yourself**: If you try to do everything on your own without delegating, you limit your ability to leverage others' skills. This can cause you to burn out and make you vulnerable to others stepping in and taking control of your projects.
- **Failing to Assert Leadership**: If you let others take the lead or fail to make decisions, you risk losing the chance to control the outcome of a project. Without a clear leader, others might take credit for your ideas, or you could be manipulated into giving away your power.
- **Not Taking Responsibility for Outcomes**: If you fail to take credit for a success or avoid the spotlight, you leave space for others to claim your achievements. This may also cause people to underestimate you or take advantage of your reluctance to assert ownership.
- **Letting Others Overperform Without Recognition**: If you neglect to take credit for work that was done under your guidance, or fail to credit yourself where it's due, you leave an opening for others to take credit for your contributions, or they might use your lack of attention to diminish your role.
- **Being Too Transparent**: If you constantly give away all the credit and don't keep certain things close to the chest, others might exploit your transparency to undermine you. People will begin to take advantage of your openness and may manipulate you into relinquishing control of credit.
- **Allowing Others to Lead or Make Decisions**: By taking a passive approach and allowing others to make decisions or take the reins, you risk them

positioning themselves as the ones responsible for the results. If you aren't the one leading, you're vulnerable to being overshadowed.

- **Being Overly Generous with Praise**: Excessively praising others for their work without ensuring that you also get your due credit can make people feel entitled to take credit for more of the work. By overly praising others, you diminish your ability to assert your own influence and recognition.

- **Not Protecting Your Ideas**: If you share your ideas too freely with others without claiming ownership or setting boundaries, people may take them and run with them. If you aren't careful, someone else might execute your ideas and take all the credit for them.

- **Giving Credit in Public, but Not Taking It**: If you give away too much credit publicly without taking ownership of the outcome, you can be manipulated into giving others the upper hand. When you're too generous with public acknowledgment and not selective about how credit is distributed, others may gain the power to influence or control you.

- **Ignoring the Strategic Value of Work Done by Others**: If you fail to recognize the strategic importance of delegating and controlling the narrative of who does the work, you risk losing credit for your efforts. Letting others take on tasks without an overarching vision can make you invisible and leave you open to manipulation by those who step in to claim the credit.

Law— **8**

Make Other People Come to You – Use Bait if Necessary

"Let your worth attract the right opportunities; don't chase what's beneath you."

— *Donesta*

Law 8: Make Other People Come to You – Use Bait if Necessary

This law encourages creating situations where others feel compelled to seek you out. By positioning yourself as valuable, you become a focal point, drawing others to you rather than expending energy pursuing them.

The Power Behind the Principle

When people come to you, they're often more willing to accept your terms. This positions you as a central figure and can amplify your influence over them. The benefit is conserving energy while reinforcing your importance and control in the dynamic.

Putting It to Use

- **Create Scarcity**: Make your time, attention, or resources appear limited. People are drawn to what they cannot easily obtain. By creating a sense of scarcity, you increase your value and make others come to you in pursuit of what they can't get elsewhere.
- **Position Yourself as a Gatekeeper**: Be the person who holds the key to important resources, opportunities, or information. People will have to come to you if they want access to what you control, whether it's a network, knowledge, or a specific skill set.
- **Leverage Your Expertise**: Cultivate a reputation for having specialized knowledge or skills that others need. When people see you as an expert in a field, they'll naturally be drawn to seek your guidance, advice, or assistance.
- **Be Hard to Reach (But Not Too Much)**: Limit your availability to create an air of mystery and importance. Make others chase after you, but don't be completely unavailable, or you risk losing their interest entirely. The key is balance—make them earn your attention, but don't make it impossible to get.
- **Use Invitations and Exclusivity**: Offer invitations to exclusive events, meetings, or gatherings that only certain people can attend. By making people feel privileged to be around you, they'll be eager to come to you, increasing your perceived value and influence.

- **Cultivate an Attractive Persona**: Develop an aura of intrigue or fascination around you. Whether it's through your appearance, charisma, or aura of success, make sure that others want to be around you or be in your circle. People will naturally want to „come to you" because they see something they want to be a part of.
- **Make Others Work for Your Attention**: Don't give away your time or attention too freely. Instead, make people prove that they are worthy of it, whether by offering something valuable in return or by showing you that they understand your worth. People will come to you if they see that you hold the power in the relationship.
- **Offer Limited Opportunities**: Create situations where people feel they have a limited window of opportunity to get something from you—whether it's a business opportunity, a meeting, or even just your advice. This urgency will push others to approach you more quickly.
- **Enhance Your Social Proof**: Build a network of influential or respected people around you. When others see that you have the backing of powerful or high-status individuals, they will want to come to you to be a part of your circle or to gain access to your connections.
- **Frame Yourself as a Respected Authority**: Position yourself as a respected figure in your industry or social circle. When you have a reputation of influence or success, people will naturally come to you for guidance, opportunities, or simply to be in your presence.

Recognizing When Others Use It

- They withhold information or resources others need.
- They create situations where others have to approach them for help.
- They make themselves scarce or hard to reach.
- They respond selectively, increasing their perceived value.
- They build a reputation for expertise in critical areas.
- They subtly indicate they're in demand or occupied.
- They keep discussions high-level until approached for specifics.
- They create dependencies by being the "go-to" person for certain tasks.
- They offer help only when directly asked.
- They signal that their time and resources are limited.

How to Neutralize Its Use

- Build your own resources and knowledge to reduce dependency.
- Approach them with clear, concise requests to save time.
- Be proactive in finding alternative solutions.
- Establish a network of contacts to reduce reliance on one person.
- Maintain a professional distance while securing necessary resources.
- Document interactions for clarity and future reference.
- Focus on developing self-sufficiency in needed areas.
- Politely but confidently address any delays or barriers.
- Emphasize collaboration rather than dependence.
- Seek mentorship or guidance from multiple sources.

Behaviors that Make You a Target

- **Chasing After Others**: If you constantly pursue others for their time, attention, or approval, you're giving away your power. When you chase people, you create an imbalance where others can control the terms of engagement. They'll manipulate you into proving your worth.
- **Offering Unsolicited Help**: Constantly offering help or advice without being asked for it can position you as someone who is overly eager to please, and others may take advantage of that. They may start expecting your assistance without reciprocating or respecting your boundaries.
- **Being Too Available**: If you make yourself too accessible, people will take your time and energy for granted. When you're always available and constantly present, people won't feel the need to work for your attention, and your perceived value will decrease.
- **Focusing Too Much on Others' Needs**: If you focus solely on others' needs and desires without asserting your own, you risk becoming a servant to them. People will come to you only when they need something, and you will be manipulated into always providing without receiving anything in return.
- **Lack of Boundaries**: If you don't set clear boundaries about when and how people can interact with you, you allow them to dictate the terms. Without boundaries, others can manipulate your time and energy, making you the one who is constantly running after others.
- **Giving Away Power Too Freely**: If you freely offer power or recognition to others without making them earn it, you lose control. When you make others

feel too comfortable in your presence, they may start taking advantage of your generosity, leaving you with little to show for your efforts.

- **Appearing Desperate for Attention**: If you act desperate for others' attention or approval, you become easily manipulated. Desperation signals to others that you are willing to do whatever it takes to gain their favor, which can lead them to take advantage of your vulnerabilities.
- **Allowing Others to Control the Agenda**: If you always allow others to dictate the pace and direction of interactions, meetings, or projects, you're ceding control. When people realize they can lead the conversation or control the flow, they can manipulate you into doing things on their terms.
- **Being Easily Influenced**: If you constantly shift your opinions or actions based on what others say or think, people will see you as easily manipulated. When you let others steer the conversation or decisions, you're giving away your power and making it easier for them to exploit you.
- **Over-Explaining Your Motives**: If you feel the need to justify every decision or action, you make yourself vulnerable to being manipulated. People can use your explanations against you or twist your words to influence your actions in ways that benefit them.

Law— **9**

Win Through Your Actions, Never Through Argument

"Your results will echo louder than your words; let your achievements do the convincing."

— *Petronis*

Law 9: Win Through Your Actions, Never Through Argument

This law encourages demonstrating competence and value through action rather than engaging in verbal disputes. Actions are tangible and difficult to dispute, while arguments often lead to defensive attitudes and resistance.

The Power Behind the Principle

Actions are undeniable and have a lasting impact, while arguments can be dismissed or countered. By proving your point through results, you gain respect and avoid unnecessary confrontations. The benefit is that others are more likely to recognize your contributions without feeling defensive or resentful.

Putting It to Use

- **Let Results Speak for Themselves**: Rather than debating your capabilities or merits, focus on producing results. Success in your actions will serve as the strongest argument, and people will naturally recognize your worth based on what you've achieved.
- **Demonstrate Leadership through Action**: Be proactive in addressing challenges or leading projects. People are more likely to follow you and respect you when you show them what you can do, rather than telling them what you know.
- **Avoid Unnecessary Disputes**: Don't engage in pointless arguments where you'll only wear down your energy and credibility. Instead, choose to act decisively and let your work or your success in the situation prove your position.
- **Be Consistent in Your Efforts**: Consistency in your actions will build trust and respect. Over time, people will see that you are reliable and capable, even if you don't argue or explain yourself constantly. Your reputation will grow through what you do.
- **Lead by Example**: Inspire others by embodying the behaviors, values, and actions that you wish to see in others. When you demonstrate the way forward through your actions, you naturally draw people to your side.
- **Create Tangible Achievements**: Rather than engaging in theoretical discussions, focus on delivering tangible outcomes. Whether it's completing

a project, solving a problem, or making progress in an area, concrete results speak louder than words.

- **Show Your Skills Through Practice, Not Theory**: Rather than trying to explain your abilities or knowledge, showcase them by putting them into practice. Demonstrating competence through action is far more convincing than any argument or explanation.
- **Silence Your Critics with Success**: If you face criticism or doubt, let your actions do the talking. Rather than defending yourself with words, outperform expectations and let the results put an end to any arguments against you.
- **Focus on Problem-Solving, Not Blaming**: When faced with issues, focus on practical solutions and actions to resolve them, rather than getting into arguments about who's right or wrong. The act of solving problems shows competence, while arguing just wastes time.
- **Take Decisive Action**: When you see an opportunity or face a challenge, take decisive, effective steps to address it. Bold action makes a stronger statement than any verbal explanation, and it will make you appear confident and in control.

Recognizing When Others Use It

- They rarely engage in debates or verbal conflicts.
- They prefer to demonstrate their points through tangible outcomes.
- They avoid getting drawn into heated discussions.
- They remain calm in the face of provocation.
- They subtly demonstrate superiority through actions.
- They focus on their work rather than justifying their methods.
- They ignore verbal challenges and proceed with their plans.
- They let their success speak for itself without seeking validation.
- They avoid confrontational situations altogether.
- They consistently deliver strong results as a form of persuasion.

How to Neutralize Its Use

- Focus on measurable achievements to reinforce your own standing.
- Avoid provoking them verbally; instead, observe their actions.
- Maintain calm and professional responses to provocations.

- Document your contributions objectively to assert value.
- Look to emulate action-based persuasion in your interactions.
- Focus on constructive collaboration rather than competition.
- Avoid unnecessary verbal defenses; let your work speak.
- Build alliances that recognize tangible contributions.
- Refrain from escalating disagreements into confrontations.
- Stay aware of any strategic actions they may use to influence outcomes.

Behaviors that Make You a Target

- **Arguing for the Sake of Arguing**: Engaging in debates or arguments for the sake of proving yourself can make you appear insecure or overly defensive. People will recognize this as a tactic to cover up weaknesses, which makes you more vulnerable to manipulation.
- **Constantly Explaining Yourself**: Over-explaining your actions or justifying your decisions can make you seem unsure or lacking in conviction. When you try to explain yourself too much, you give others the chance to question your credibility or use your words against you.
- **Failing to Back Up Claims with Action**: If you talk about your abilities, achievements, or goals but fail to follow through with action, people will see you as all talk and no substance. This makes you an easy target for manipulation, as others may start questioning your intentions.
- **Engaging in Power Struggles**: Constantly trying to prove you're right through argument or confrontation can lead to conflict, which will drain your energy and focus. Manipulators thrive in these situations because they can exploit your emotional reactions to control the narrative.
- **Over-Defending Your Position**: If you find yourself constantly defending your views or actions, it suggests that you're uncertain or insecure. Manipulators will use this tendency to attack your position, knowing they can destabilize your confidence and influence.
- **Involving Others in Disputes**: When you get involved in public arguments or bring others into your conflicts, you risk losing control of the situation. People can use your disputes to manipulate you by creating divisions or pitting you against others.
- **Chasing Validation Through Words**: If you constantly seek validation or approval through verbal arguments, you make yourself vulnerable to

manipulation. People who know you need this validation can exploit it to control you or take advantage of your desire to be acknowledged.

- **Allowing Yourself to Be Dragged into Drama**: If you're frequently involved in arguments or dramatic situations, others can manipulate you into wasting your energy on these distractions. Drama diverts your attention from real work and makes you susceptible to exploitation.
- **Relying on Logic Over Action**: Constantly arguing your point with logic and reason, while neglecting to act on your plans, will make you appear ineffective. Manipulators will take advantage of this by using your inaction to steer the situation in their favor.
- **Letting Others Define Your Worth**: If you find yourself defending your value or status to others, you allow them to control the narrative. Manipulators may use this vulnerability to assert their own power, making you work harder to prove yourself without getting any recognition.

Law— **10**

Infection: Avoid the Unhappy and Unlucky

"Surround yourself only with people who are going to lift you higher."

— Oprah Winfrey

Law 10: Infection: Avoid the Unhappy and Unlucky

This law advises steering clear of people who are habitually negative, unhappy, or unlucky, as their misfortune and outlook can spread and affect your own prospects. Associating with negativity can weigh you down and compromise your progress.

The Power Behind the Principle

Negativity is often contagious; by surrounding yourself with positive, capable individuals, you maintain a healthy and motivating environment. The benefit is protecting your mental well-being and focusing on constructive relationships that support your growth.

Putting It to Use

- **Choose Your Associations Carefully**: Be mindful of the people you spend time with. Surround yourself with those who are successful, optimistic, and productive, as they will uplift you and enhance your own opportunities for success.
- **Distance Yourself from Negative People**: If someone consistently exudes negativity, whether in their outlook on life, work, or relationships, distance yourself. Their pessimism can influence your own mindset, potentially undermining your energy and motivation.
- **Seek Out Positive, High-Energy Individuals**: Make a habit of seeking relationships with those who inspire you, encourage your growth, and bring enthusiasm to your endeavors. High-energy individuals will lift you up and open doors you might not even see.
- **Avoid the Perpetual Victim**: People who constantly complain, blame others, or see themselves as victims are toxic for your personal and professional growth. These individuals will drag you down with their negative perspective and prevent you from moving forward.
- **Identify and Avoid Emotional Drainers**: Emotional vampires—people who demand constant attention, sympathy, or energy—can leave you exhausted and uninspired. Avoid getting drawn into their drama or feeling obligated to "fix" their problems.

- **Align with People Who Bring Opportunities**: Focus on relationships with individuals who can open doors or help you achieve your goals, whether through their expertise, network, or resources. Their positive outcomes will create positive momentum for you as well.
- **Recognize the Power of Group Dynamics**: Pay attention to the general mood and attitude of the groups you are part of. If the group is consistently negative or stuck in a cycle of failure, it will affect your own mindset and progress. Shift your focus to groups that are thriving and moving forward.
- **Set Boundaries with Toxic People**: It's important to set clear boundaries with people who bring negativity into your life. Politely disengage from conversations or situations where their negativity is being spread, and don't allow their energy to derail your focus.
- **Learn to Let Go of Unhealthy Relationships**: Sometimes it's necessary to cut ties with people who have become a drag on your personal or professional life. If someone consistently brings you down or makes you feel drained, it's better to distance yourself rather than prolong a damaging relationship.
- **Cultivate Self-Awareness**: Be aware of how different people make you feel after you interact with them. If you feel drained, disillusioned, or pessimistic, consider whether you need to spend less time with that person. Your own energy is precious, and you should guard it wisely.

Recognizing When Others Use It

- They avoid relationships with overly negative people.
- They limit interactions with those who frequently complain.
- They don't get involved in others' personal issues or misfortunes.
- They align with people who exhibit a positive attitude.
- They avoid discussing their own problems around others.
- They seem unaffected by gossip or pessimism.
- They distance themselves from people who bring chaos or drama.
- They focus on productive, positive conversations.
- They consistently choose friends and colleagues wisely.
- They change the subject or disengage when negativity arises.

How to Neutralize Its Use

- Evaluate your own mindset to ensure you project positivity.
- Avoid discussing negative events in detail with colleagues.
- Build a circle of optimistic, solution-oriented individuals.
- Focus on positive, forward-thinking topics in discussions.
- Limit time spent with those who frequently dwell on problems.
- Encourage constructive feedback rather than complaints.
- Be proactive in addressing your own challenges privately.
- Offer solutions when discussing problems to avoid complaining.
- Be open to advice from positive influences.
- Avoid mirroring negativity; stay neutral in difficult situations.

Behaviors that Make You a Target

- **Allowing Yourself to Be Surrounded by Negative Influences**: If you spend time with people who are always complaining, doubting, or failing, you risk adopting their mindset. Their negativity can subtly shift your own perspective, leading you to feel defeated or pessimistic about your own goals.
- **Getting Involved in Other People's Drama**: Engaging in other people's emotional problems or crises can pull you into their world of negativity. If you consistently allow yourself to be caught up in the misfortunes or personal struggles of others, you may become entangled in their problems and unable to focus on your own success.
- **Becoming Overly Empathetic Toward the Unlucky**: While empathy is important, being overly empathetic with those who are constantly unlucky or unsuccessful can drag you down. If you spend too much emotional energy trying to help someone who isn't helping themselves, it may weaken your ability to move forward with your own goals.
- **Staying Loyal to a Failing Group**: Loyalty is a valuable trait, but if you're loyal to a group that is constantly struggling or stuck in a cycle of failure, it can hurt you. You may waste time and energy trying to support others without gaining any benefits in return, or worse, find yourself caught in the group's stagnation.
- **Ignoring Red Flags in Relationships**: If you overlook warning signs about a person's negative energy, toxic behavior, or consistent bad luck, you may be allowing them to manipulate you into wasting your time or resources. This

could include people who prey on your desire to help them but never take responsibility for improving their situation.

- **Engaging in Victimhood Mentality**: If you yourself adopt a victim mentality, you might inadvertently attract other people with similar attitudes. This creates a cycle of negativity and can cause you to focus on what's wrong rather than what can be done to improve your situation.
- **Chasing Unavailable or Unsuccessful Individuals**: Whether in relationships or professional settings, pursuing people who are emotionally unavailable, unsuccessful, or unable to reciprocate your efforts leads to frustration and self-doubt. Manipulative individuals may take advantage of your attention without offering anything in return.
- **Becoming a Fixer**: If you make a habit of trying to „fix" others—especially those who are chronically unlucky or unhappy—you set yourself up for emotional manipulation. They may use your desire to help them to gain your support without ever making meaningful changes in their own lives.
- **Getting Stuck in Other People's Failures**: If you spend too much time focusing on or worrying about others' failures, you may end up repeating their mistakes. Instead of learning from their setbacks, you might inadvertently internalize their negative beliefs or habits, which will hold you back.
- **Focusing on Pleasing the Unhappy**: If you're constantly trying to please or make the unhappy people around you feel better, it can drain your energy and focus. These individuals may manipulate your emotions to get attention, sympathy, or resources without ever offering anything in return.

Part III

Navigating Relationships and Office Politics

Law 11: Learn to Keep People Dependent on You
Build your value so others can't imagine succeeding without you.

Law 12: Use Selective Honesty and Generosity to Disarm Your Victim
Earn trust strategically to gain the upper hand.

Law 13: When Asking for Help, Appeal to People's Self-Interest, Never to Their Mercy or Gratitude
Frame your requests in terms of others' benefits.

Law 14: Pose as a Friend, Work as a Spy
Gather the information you need without revealing too much.

Law 15: Crush Your Enemy Totally
End power struggles decisively to avoid future challenges.

Law— **11**

Learn to Keep People Dependent on You

"The best way to keep power is to make sure people need you."

— Niccolò Machiavelli

Law 11: Learn to Keep People Dependent on You

This law suggests making others reliant on you to maintain power and influence. By positioning yourself as an indispensable asset, you secure your place and make it difficult for others to proceed without you.

The Power Behind the Principle

Dependency reduces the likelihood of opposition and increases loyalty. When people rely on you, they are less inclined to challenge you and more likely to protect your position. The benefit is security and control, as well as reduced competition.

Putting It to Use

- **Cultivate Unique Skills or Knowledge**: Develop specialized skills, expertise, or knowledge that others cannot easily replicate. By becoming the go-to person for something rare or valuable, you ensure that people need you in order to gain access to that skill or information.
- **Be the Gatekeeper of Resources**: Control access to valuable resources, whether it's information, connections, or material goods. If others depend on you to get these resources, you position yourself as someone they can't afford to ignore.
- **Create Dependency Through Emotional Investment**: Build strong emotional ties with others, whether through support, guidance, or mentorship. When people become emotionally invested in you, they may feel obligated to rely on you for reassurance or validation, making them more dependent on your presence or approval.
- **Provide Exclusive Access to Opportunities**: Make yourself the gatekeeper to exclusive opportunities, whether they be job offers, networking events, or critical business information. By offering access to opportunities others can't get on their own, you create a dependency on your ability to open doors.
- **Deliver Results That Others Can't Match**: Consistently outperform others in ways that they can't easily replicate. By being the best in your field or delivering exceptional results, others will come to rely on you for your expertise or leadership, making you indispensable.

- **Build Strategic Alliances**: Form relationships with influential individuals and use these connections to create dependency. When people know that you have the ear of powerful figures or access to key decision-makers, they will depend on you to mediate or advance their interests.
- **Make Yourself the Source of Vital Information**: Position yourself as the person who holds critical information that others need. By being the one who can provide insights, answers, or strategies that others can't easily access, you ensure that people remain reliant on you for direction and knowledge.
- **Create a Personal Brand or Reputation**: Cultivate a personal brand or reputation for excellence, reliability, or indispensability. If people come to view you as a critical figure in your field or circle, they will be more likely to depend on you, seeking your guidance, approval, or leadership.
- **Offer Help, but in a Way That Makes Others Need You**: Help others solve problems or achieve goals, but do so in a way that leaves them reliant on your continued support. For example, offer solutions that require follow-up or long-term collaboration, ensuring that people will continue to need your involvement.
- **Be the Master of Deliberate Control**: Control the pace of progress and the flow of information. By keeping others in a state of uncertainty about next steps or outcomes, you increase their dependence on your decisions and actions to move things forward.

Recognizing When Others Use It

- They position themselves as the sole source of certain knowledge.
- They frequently offer exclusive expertise or skills.
- They keep critical information private or guarded.
- They volunteer for roles others are less familiar with.
- They discourage others from developing similar skills.
- They provide selective help, ensuring people return to them.
- They emphasize their contributions in key areas.
- They avoid sharing their methods in detail.
- They cultivate strong relationships with key decision-makers.
- They subtly highlight their importance to the group's success.

How to Neutralize Its Use

- Develop multiple skills to avoid over-reliance on one person.
- Document your processes to ensure continuity.
- Learn and understand key areas relevant to your role.
- Share knowledge openly to reduce dependency.
- Encourage others to develop overlapping expertise.
- Build relationships with multiple key contacts.
- Observe and document any practices that create dependency.
- Seek out training to broaden your skill set.
- Collaborate with others to share knowledge collectively.
- Avoid placing yourself in a single point of reliance.

Behaviors that Make You a Target

- **Being Too Independent or Self-Sufficient**: If you always do everything on your own and don't need anyone, you can alienate others or miss opportunities to form useful dependencies. By being overly self-sufficient, you may fail to position yourself as someone others would seek out for help, leaving you open to being manipulated by those who know how to control others.
- **Failing to Set Boundaries**: If you don't set clear boundaries or limit the extent to which people can depend on you, you invite others to take advantage of your time, resources, or energy. People will manipulate you into becoming overly involved in their problems or making you the default solution to their issues.
- **Being Too Generous with Your Time and Resources**: When you give too freely of your time, attention, or resources without ensuring a reciprocal relationship, you create an imbalance where people may become dependent on you without offering anything of value in return. This invites manipulation, as others will take your generosity for granted.
- **Letting Others Rely on You for Validation**: If you let others constantly seek your validation or approval, you place yourself in a situation where they become emotionally dependent on you. This makes you vulnerable to manipulation, as people can use your approval to control your actions or opinions.

- **Over-Explaining or Over-Justifying Yourself**: Constantly explaining yourself or justifying your actions to others can create a sense of dependence. People might start relying on you to justify decisions or offer explanations, which gives them power over you by controlling the narrative.
- **Taking on the Role of the „Fixer"**: If you consistently take on the role of solving other people's problems, you can make them dependent on you to address their issues. This may lead them to manipulate your time and energy, expecting you to always be the one to come to the rescue.
- **Becoming a Source of Drama or Uncertainty**: If you create unnecessary drama or confusion in your relationships, people may begin to rely on you to resolve it, thereby increasing their dependence on you. Manipulative people may exploit this uncertainty to gain control over you, keeping you in a constant state of dependence.
- **Failing to Establish Your Own Power Base**: If you don't have a network, resources, or personal leverage that you can fall back on, you may create an unhealthy reliance on others. By not establishing your own independent power base, you become susceptible to those who will manipulate you in order to maintain control over you.
- **Avoiding Conflict or Hard Conversations**: If you avoid conflict or tough conversations in relationships, others will begin to rely on you to maintain harmony or be the peacemaker. This makes you dependent on their approval or actions, leaving you open to manipulation from those who know how to use this dynamic.
- **Lack of Assertiveness in Relationships**: If you don't assert your needs or desires, others may begin to take advantage of your passive nature. This creates a situation where people depend on you to accommodate them, which can be manipulated into controlling or exploiting your time, energy, and efforts.

Law— **12**

Use Selective Honesty and Generosity to Disarm Your Victim

"No legacy is so rich as honesty."

— William Shakespeare

Law 12: Use Selective Honesty and Generosity to Disarm Your Victim

This law advises using small acts of honesty or generosity to gain trust, making others let down their guard. These gestures create a perception of goodwill, allowing for influence and manipulation when needed.

The Power Behind the Principle

People are more likely to trust those who demonstrate kindness or transparency. By selectively being honest or generous, you create an illusion of trustworthiness, which can be leveraged for influence. The benefit is increased influence and reduced suspicion in future interactions.

Putting It to Use

- **Give a Small Gift or Gesture**: Offer a token of generosity—something small and thoughtful but not too extravagant. By giving a seemingly selfless gesture, you can build goodwill and create an impression of kindness, which you can later leverage when you need something in return.
- **Be Transparent About Your Intentions (Sometimes)**: Be genuinely honest about your intentions in certain situations, but don't reveal everything. A well-placed moment of transparency can make people believe you are sincere, which can disarm their defenses and make them more vulnerable to your influence.
- **Share Personal Information (But Selectively)**: Occasionally share personal stories or experiences to create a sense of intimacy and trust. This vulnerability makes people feel closer to you, allowing you to manipulate the emotional bond for your own benefit without oversharing and losing control.
- **Appeal to Emotions with Generosity**: Act generously at a moment when someone is emotionally vulnerable or in need. This generosity can create a strong bond, making the other person more likely to be influenced or manipulated by you when you ask for something later.
- **Give Praise or Compliments with a Purpose**: Give sincere, targeted compliments that flatter others and make them feel good about themselves. This can disarm any suspicion they might have and put them in a more

receptive, trusting frame of mind, making it easier to manipulate the situation in your favor.

- **Help in Times of Need**: Offer assistance when someone is going through a rough patch or a difficult time. This act of kindness can generate a sense of gratitude, causing the person to feel indebted to you, which gives you leverage when you need something later.

- **Appear Humble and Self-Sacrificing**: Occasionally act humble or self-sacrificing in a situation to create the appearance of having no ulterior motives. People who see you as a humble, unselfish person are less likely to suspect that you are using them for your own gain.

- **Throw In a Moment of Brutal Honesty**: Deliver a truth that is unexpected, but strategically useful. A brutal but genuine admission can make people trust you more, lowering their guard. This vulnerability will also give you an opportunity to introduce your own needs, which they will be more likely to accept or support.

- **Make Others Feel Special**: Show people that they are important by giving them attention or a special favor. This will make them feel valued and more inclined to trust you. Once you've built this rapport, you can use it to subtly manipulate them to your advantage.

- **Create a Debt of Gratitude**: Be generous in ways that make the other person feel indebted to you, even if the gift is small. When you give generously without immediately asking for something in return, you lay the foundation for future influence, as the other person will feel a need to reciprocate.

Recognizing When Others Use It

- They give unexpected gifts or praise without clear reason.
- They reveal small vulnerabilities to seem approachable.
- They occasionally admit minor faults or mistakes.
- They offer generous help or resources on select occasions.
- They use flattery in a subtle, non-intrusive way.
- They disclose personal stories to create a sense of trust.
- They make visible, deliberate efforts to seem transparent.
- They do favors that put others at ease.
- They acknowledge others' strengths openly.
- They encourage others to reciprocate trust.

How to Neutralize Its Use

- Be mindful of overly generous acts; question the motive if unsure.
- Focus on observing consistent patterns rather than isolated actions.
- Stay neutral in response to praise or gifts.
- Maintain professional boundaries despite friendly gestures.
- Encourage transparency and fair reciprocity.
- Keep records of favors or agreements to avoid misunderstandings.
- Avoid reciprocating too quickly in a way that creates dependence.
- Stay consistent in professional interactions.
- Assess past interactions to gauge reliability.
- Avoid assuming all gestures are without self-interest.

Behaviors that Make You a Target

- Being Too Open and Transparent: If you overshare or constantly expose your true intentions, you can make yourself too predictable and vulnerable. Manipulative individuals will use this honesty to gain control of your actions or turn your openness into a weakness.
- Giving Without a Clear Boundary: If you give too much without any clear expectation of reciprocity, you risk being taken advantage of. While generosity can build trust, a manipulative person might see your giving nature as an opportunity to extract more from you without ever offering anything in return.
- Lacking Discernment in Who You Trust: If you trust people too easily and without caution, they can use your openness against you. Manipulators often present themselves as trustworthy and generous, only to later exploit your trust and vulnerability for their gain.
- Being Too Predictable with Your Generosity: If you are always the first to offer help, praise, or generosity, others may begin to take you for granted. A manipulative person will start relying on your kindness as a constant resource, making you easier to control or deceive.
- Falling for Flattery: If you are too easily influenced by compliments or praise, you open yourself up to manipulation. Flattery can be used as a tool to lower your defenses, making you more susceptible to being swayed by others who are only interested in using you.

- Being Excessively Emotional: Showing too much emotional vulnerability can give others the opportunity to exploit your feelings. If you are constantly emotionally open, you risk being manipulated by people who will use your emotions to get what they want.
- Making Yourself Too Available: If you are always available to others, offering help, advice, or support at every turn, you may be seen as a resource to be drained. Manipulators take advantage of people who are eager to help, knowing they can get more from you by keeping you in a state of constant availability.
- Seeking Constant Validation: If you're constantly seeking validation or approval, you make yourself susceptible to being manipulated through selective honesty or praise. A manipulative person can exploit your need for validation by giving you just enough positive feedback to keep you hooked.
- Giving Without Discernment: If you give to people without considering their true motives or your own needs, you become vulnerable. Generosity can be used as a tool for manipulation if you fail to protect your own interests and only focus on pleasing others.
- Being Too Honest and Transparent with Your Weaknesses: If you openly expose your weaknesses or insecurities, people can use this against you. A manipulative individual will notice these vulnerabilities and exploit them, knowing how to press your emotional buttons or take advantage of your trust.

Law— **13**

When Asking for Help, Appeal to People's Self-Interest, Never to Their Mercy or Gratitude

---

"When a man tells you he got rich through hard work, ask him whose."

— Don Marquis

Law 13: When Asking for Help, Appeal to People's Self-Interest, Never to Their Mercy or Gratitude

This law suggests that when seeking help, it's more effective to appeal to others' self-interest rather than relying on appeals to kindness or gratitude. People are more inclined to act when they see a benefit for themselves.

The Power Behind the Principle

People are often driven by personal incentives rather than altruism. By appealing to what benefits them, you increase the likelihood of their cooperation. The benefit is a stronger influence and the ability to inspire others to act in ways that align with your goals.

Putting It to Use

- **Highlight Mutual Benefits**: When asking for assistance, frame your request in terms of what the other person stands to gain. For example, show how your success or the success of the project will also benefit them. People are more likely to help if they see how it aligns with their own interests.
- **Create Win-Win Scenarios**: Always present your request as an opportunity for collaboration, where both parties benefit. This can be done by highlighting how helping you can help them achieve their own goals, expand their network, or gain a competitive advantage.
- **Appeal to Their Ambition**: Appeal to the other person's desires for power, status, or achievement. If you can show how helping you will advance their own personal or professional goals, they are more likely to be motivated to assist you.
- **Show How They Will Look Good by Helping**: People often act out of a desire to improve their own reputation or status. When asking for help, make it clear how their involvement will reflect well on them, whether it's through public recognition, improved social standing, or strengthening their own network.
- **Offer Something in Return (or the Promise of Future Gains)**: While you may not be able to repay someone immediately, let them know that helping

you now will be rewarded later. This can be in the form of future favors, introductions, or other resources they might value in the future.

- **Use Flattery to Align Their Interests with Yours**: Appeal to their self-image by flattering them or acknowledging their expertise, position, or reputation. People like to feel important and valuable, so letting them know how their help will reflect their skills or knowledge can motivate them to act in their own self-interest.
- **Make Your Request Timely**: Be strategic about when you ask for help. Ask for assistance when the person is most likely to benefit from it, such as when they are looking for new opportunities, need recognition, or want to position themselves advantageously.
- **Emphasize Urgency with Tangible Benefits**: When appropriate, make it clear that acting now will yield immediate, tangible benefits for the other person. The more they can see an instant payoff for their efforts, the more likely they are to help you.
- **Leverage Their Need for Influence or Control**: Some people crave control or influence over situations. By positioning your request in a way that gives them the power to affect the outcome, you make them feel important and in control, which may increase their motivation to help.
- **Align Your Needs with Their Values or Goals**: Understand what the other person values, whether it's financial success, social prestige, or personal growth, and frame your request in a way that demonstrates how helping you will support those values or goals. The more you align with their personal objectives, the more they will be inclined to assist you.

Recognizing When Others Use It

- They frame requests in terms of mutual benefits.
- They often highlight how helping them will benefit the other party.
- They avoid asking for favors based purely on goodwill.
- They offer incentives or rewards when seeking assistance.
- They emphasize alignment with the other person's interests.
- They make the request seem mutually advantageous.
- They avoid discussing personal needs, focusing on shared goals.
- They downplay the favor as a collaborative effort.
- They build the request around the other person's priorities.
- They often present their requests in business-like terms.

How to Neutralize Its Use

- Consider the request's benefits to ensure they're genuine.
- Clarify any potential expectations attached to the help.
- Determine if the request aligns with your own goals.
- Set clear boundaries on the level of help you provide.
- Be cautious of ulterior motives disguised as mutual benefit.
- Ask for specific details on the request's potential outcomes.
- Avoid committing if the arrangement seems one-sided.
- Assess whether the favor truly benefits both parties equally.
- Politely decline if you feel pressured into acting.
- Remain professional and objective in evaluating the request.

Behaviors that Make You a Target

- **Appealing to Their Mercy or Gratitude**: If you ask for help based on a sense of obligation or mercy, rather than on what benefits the other person, you risk appearing weak or needy. Manipulative individuals can exploit this vulnerability, using your dependence or emotional appeal to gain leverage over you.
- **Focusing on Emotional Pleas**: Relying too much on emotions—such as guilt, pity, or gratitude—when asking for help puts you in a position of weakness. People may help out of obligation, but they are less likely to do so for the right reasons, making you vulnerable to manipulation.
- **Failing to Make It Clear What's In It for Them**: If you don't articulate how helping you will benefit the other person, they may feel no incentive to assist you. When you fail to show how your request aligns with their self-interest, people may either refuse to help or only do so out of politeness, leaving you vulnerable to being manipulated in return.
- **Over-Explaining or Justifying Yourself**: If you find yourself over-explaining why you need help or justifying your request repeatedly, it signals insecurity. Manipulative individuals can use this weakness to push you into a situation where you become indebted to them, or they can exploit your desperation for assistance.
- **Being Too Dependent on Others**: Constantly relying on others to help you without offering something in return makes you vulnerable to manipulation. If people perceive you as someone who always needs assistance, they may

offer help but only in exchange for something they can later use to control or manipulate you.

- **Giving Too Much Power to the Other Person**: If you give too much control or decision-making power to the person you are asking for help, you may inadvertently set yourself up for manipulation. Instead of empowering them through your request, you become dependent on their actions, which could be used to sway or influence your decisions in the future.

- **Appearing to Have No Alternatives**: If you make it seem like you have no other options and that this person is your only source of help, you can create a power imbalance that invites manipulation. People may feel they have the upper hand and use your vulnerability to manipulate you.

- **Failing to Establish Reciprocity**: If you don't establish that your request for help is part of a mutually beneficial relationship or fail to offer something in return, you invite the other person to take advantage of you. Without a sense of balance, your relationships can become transactional, and manipulators can take advantage of this imbalance.

- **Being Too Indirect or Hesitant in Your Request**: If you hesitate or don't clearly state your needs, you give the other person an opportunity to take advantage of your indecisiveness. People may use your lack of clarity to pressurize you into agreeing to their terms or manipulating you into doing something that doesn't benefit you.

- **Ignoring the Other Person's Interests or Needs**: If you ask for help without considering what the other person wants or needs in return, they may feel exploited or unappreciated. Manipulative individuals will exploit this oversight, taking advantage of your failure to engage their self-interest and using your lack of consideration against you.

Law — **14**

Pose as a Friend, Work as a Spy

"Be observant and insightful, gathering wisdom that others freely reveal."

— *Xi Liam*

Law 14: Pose as a Friend, Work as a Spy

This law advises gaining insight by positioning yourself as a friendly confidant. By appearing to be a supportive ally, you can gather valuable information that may benefit you later.

The Power Behind the Principle

People are more likely to reveal information to those they trust. By building rapport, you gain access to knowledge and insights that can be used strategically. The benefit is that you remain informed, which gives you leverage in future interactions or negotiations.

Putting It to Use

- **Build Trust by Offering Support**: Present yourself as a supportive and helpful person to those you wish to gather information from. Be generous with advice, lend a listening ear, or offer your help on projects. This creates a bond of trust, allowing you to gather details without raising suspicion.
- **Listen More Than You Speak**: In conversations, adopt the strategy of listening more than speaking. People will often reveal valuable information when they feel heard and understood. Your position as a listener allows you to gather insights without giving away too much about your own intentions.
- **Appeal to Their Emotions**: By showing genuine empathy and concern for others' feelings or challenges, you can get them to open up about their plans, goals, or vulnerabilities. Appearing emotionally attuned makes people comfortable with sharing information they might otherwise keep to themselves.
- **Flatter and Compliment**: Use flattery to make people feel good about themselves. Compliment their ideas, skills, or achievements. This makes them feel safe and valued, which can lead to them revealing more than they normally would, including sensitive or strategic information.
- **Be Inquisitive (But Subtle)**: When interacting with others, ask open-ended questions that encourage them to share more about their personal and professional lives. Be subtle and nonchalant in your inquiries, so they don't realize you're gathering information for a strategic purpose.

- **Offer Solutions or Advice**: Help others solve their problems in ways that benefit them, but also give you insight into their weaknesses or challenges. By presenting yourself as a helpful figure, you'll gain their trust, and over time, they may reveal information that can be used to your advantage.
- **Observe Behavior and Body Language**: Pay attention not only to what people say, but how they behave. Look for contradictions between their words and actions, and observe subtle cues in their body language. This can give you more information than what's explicitly stated, helping you gauge their true motives.
- **Share Personal Information to Create Reciprocity**: Share minor personal details or opinions to foster a sense of mutual exchange. When you make people feel that they are getting to know you, they will feel more inclined to open up and share details about themselves in return.
- **Use Social Situations to Gather Insights**: Take advantage of social gatherings, team meetings, or casual interactions to learn about the plans and intentions of others. Informal environments are often where people let their guard down and speak more freely about their objectives or frustrations.
- **Keep Your Own Cards Close**: Never reveal too much about yourself or your true intentions. Keep a bit of mystery about who you really are and what you really want. The less people know about you, the more freely they will speak about themselves, and the more information you can collect.

Recognizing When Others Use It

- They often ask probing questions under the guise of interest.
- They frequently share minimal details about themselves.
- They tend to recall and reference information you've shared.
- They are consistently friendly yet somewhat guarded.
- They steer conversations to gather information indirectly.
- They show selective interest in specific topics you discuss.
- They make you feel comfortable enough to disclose.
- They rarely open up about their personal challenges.
- They tend to encourage you to talk about yourself.
- They discreetly observe your responses to gauge reactions.

How to Neutralize Its Use

- Be cautious with personal or sensitive information.
- Keep conversations neutral and professional.
- Share minimal information, especially about weaknesses.
- Maintain boundaries without appearing distrustful.
- Ask open-ended questions to assess their motives.
- Limit discussions on topics they seem overly interested in.
- Refrain from discussing goals and strategies in detail.
- Observe their reactions to gauge their intent.
- Be mindful of what you disclose in casual conversations.
- Document interactions to recall details if needed.

Behaviors that Make You a Target

- **Being Overly Open About Your Own Plans**: If you share too much about your own ideas, goals, or strategies, you invite others to use that information against you. Manipulators will use your openness to gather intelligence, plan against you, or undermine your efforts while pretending to be your friend.
- **Trusting Too Easily**: If you trust others quickly and without scrutiny, you leave yourself vulnerable to those who may be posing as your friend while secretly gathering information for their own advantage. Always maintain a degree of skepticism in relationships.
- **Being Too Honest or Transparent**: If you are overly candid about your thoughts, motives, or weaknesses, you open yourself up to exploitation. Those who pose as friends may use your vulnerabilities against you in the future, taking advantage of your openness for their own gain.
- **Overlooking Subtle Cues or Red Flags**: If you fail to observe people's behavior closely or ignore contradictions in their words and actions, you may be manipulated without realizing it. People posing as friends may use this blind spot to deceive you and gather sensitive information without you noticing.
- **Focusing Only on Being Liked or Accepted**: If you're too focused on making friends and gaining acceptance, you may become too trusting and willing to share details that could be used against you. Manipulators exploit the desire to be liked by pretending to be friends while collecting information.

- **Being Too Emotional or Revealing in Casual Conversations**: If you let your emotions get the best of you in casual or friendly conversations, you may inadvertently reveal more than you intended. Manipulative people posing as friends will use these moments to gather emotional information that they can use to control or influence you.
- **Not Setting Boundaries with Others**: If you don't establish clear boundaries, people may feel comfortable prying into your personal life, while you may not even realize they're gathering information. This lack of personal boundaries invites manipulators to gather intelligence without being noticed.
- **Being Easily Flattered or Taken Advantage Of**: If you're easily influenced by compliments and flattery, you risk opening yourself up to manipulation. People who pose as friends can use flattery to gain your trust, then use the information you share to manipulate or control you.
- **Ignoring the Power Dynamics in Relationships**: If you fail to recognize that some people may be pretending to be your ally in order to gather information, you may be manipulated. People who operate as „spies" are often skilled at hiding their true intentions, and you may not notice the subtle ways they gain information from you.
- **Being Overly Helpful to Others**: If you are always the one helping and offering support without considering the other person's true motives, you may invite manipulation. Manipulators may take advantage of your helpfulness to gain your trust, all while gathering information about your plans and weaknesses.

Law— **15**

Crush Your Enemy Totally

"When you strike at a king, you must kill him."

— Ralph Waldo Emerson

Law 15: Crush Your Enemy Totally

This law advises dealing decisively with opponents, leaving no room for future retaliation or resistance. Complete victory ensures that your enemies cannot regroup or threaten you again.

The Power Behind the Principle

Partial victories often allow opponents to regroup and retaliate. A total defeat eliminates threats, creating a secure environment for future endeavors. The benefit is long-term stability, as well as reducing the potential for opposition.

Putting It to Use

- **Take Swift and Decisive Action**: When an enemy is vulnerable or making mistakes, strike quickly and decisively. Delaying your move can allow them time to recover or regroup, so ensure you act while they are still in a weak position.
- **Destroy Their Support System**: Identify and dismantle the alliances or relationships that support your enemy. If you isolate them from their resources, networks, or allies, you eliminate their ability to pose a threat, making it impossible for them to regain power.
- **Use Their Weaknesses Against Them**: Exploit your enemy's vulnerabilities to weaken their position. This could be personal flaws, professional weaknesses, or insecurities. By amplifying these weaknesses, you erode their foundation and neutralize their ability to challenge you.
- **Ensure No Room for Escape**: When defeating an opponent, leave them with no viable options to escape or recover. This means not only defeating them in battle but also blocking any exit routes—whether financial, social, or professional—that would allow them to rebuild.
- **Humiliate Them Publicly**: Publicly expose and humiliate your enemy to damage their reputation. If they lose face in front of others, it becomes much harder for them to mount a comeback or regain credibility, especially in the eyes of those who once supported them.
- **Create Unavoidable Consequences**: Make the consequences of your enemy's actions so severe and irreversible that they cannot recover. Whether

through legal, social, or economic means, ensure that their defeat leads to irreversible losses, ensuring they are too weakened to retaliate.

- **Exhaust Their Resources**: Deplete their resources—financial, emotional, or strategic—so that they no longer have the means to fight back. This could mean draining their finances, sabotaging their plans, or undermining their support, so they are left defenseless.
- **Cut Off Their Access to Power**: Stripping your enemy of their sources of power—whether it's information, support, or position—renders them impotent. Without access to what made them powerful, they lose their ability to be a threat to you or anyone else.
- **Make Sure They Have No Following Left**: After defeating your enemy, work to turn their followers or supporters against them. If you can persuade or coerce their allies to abandon them, you isolate your enemy and make it impossible for them to stage a comeback.
- **Reinforce Your Victory**: After your victory, continue to ensure that your enemy stays defeated by solidifying your position and strengthening your own power. Do not allow any breathing room for your enemy to regroup or for others to question your victory.

Recognizing When Others Use It

- They take actions that seem disproportionately strong.
- They respond decisively to minor opposition.
- They seek to eliminate all opposition completely.
- They rarely forgive or compromise with opponents.
- They act preemptively to remove potential threats.
- They cut ties completely after conflicts.
- They are unyielding in their demands during disputes.
- They show minimal tolerance for dissenting views.
- They appear determined to control all aspects of outcomes.
- They pursue goals with a "win-at-all-costs" mindset.

How to Neutralize Its Use

- Assess the risk before engaging directly with them.
- Seek alliances to counteract their influence.
- Avoid direct confrontation if unnecessary.

- Maintain a neutral stance in conflicts involving them.
- Build resilience in areas they target.
- Address concerns calmly and professionally.
- Document interactions and outcomes in case of escalation.
- Avoid appearing as a threat; focus on collaboration.
- Set boundaries without challenging their authority.
- Seek higher support if their actions become too aggressive.

Behaviors that Make You a Target

- **Underestimating Your Enemy**: If you underestimate the capabilities of an opponent, you risk leaving them with a chance to recover and retaliate. Failing to recognize the potential strength of your adversary leaves you vulnerable to future problems, which could lead to your eventual defeat.
- **Leaving Room for Negotiation**: If you offer your enemy the opportunity to negotiate or make compromises, you allow them a chance to regain power. Instead, if you crush your enemy completely, they have no room to recover or plot against you.
- **Failing to Follow Through**: If you fail to finish the job or take decisive action, your enemy can regroup and come back stronger. Incomplete actions or half-measures invite future retaliation, leaving your own position unstable.
- **Relying on Mercy or Compassion**: If you allow your enemy any mercy or compassion, you leave them with the possibility of mounting a comeback. Giving them any chance to escape or rebuild will encourage them to come back after you with renewed strength.
- **Being Too Cautious or Hesitant**: If you hesitate or show caution when you have the upper hand, you give your enemy time to recover. Indecision or delaying action allows them to regain strength, reorganize, or form new alliances.
- **Underestimating the Value of Allies**: If you don't recognize the importance of breaking your enemy's alliances or support network, they may find other resources or allies to help them recover. Failing to isolate them completely means they can rebuild and retaliate in the future.
- **Allowing Public Sympathy for Your Enemy**: If your enemy is seen as a victim or if they receive sympathy from the public or key figures, you create space for them to regain influence. By not thoroughly discrediting them, you leave open the possibility that others may support them and help them recover.

- **Being Too Generous with Your Own Resources**: If you share too much of your own resources or make concessions to your enemy, you risk weakening your position. Instead, it's better to use your resources to ensure your victory is complete, so they cannot bounce back.
- **Neglecting to Monitor Your Enemy**: If you think that your victory over an enemy is final and you stop monitoring them, you open the door for them to regroup or find new ways to challenge you. Continuous vigilance is necessary to ensure your position remains secure after a defeat.
- **Failing to Address Hidden Threats**: If you don't uncover and address all potential sources of resistance, including hidden allies or secret plans your enemy may be developing, you leave yourself open to surprise attacks or unexpected rebounds. Without fully eradicating these hidden threats, you allow your enemy to rise again.

PART IV

Elevating Your Presence

Law 16: Use Absence to Increase Respect and Honor
Step back when needed to reinforce your value.

Law 17: Keep Others in Suspended Terror: Cultivate an Air of Unpredictability
Stay one step ahead by keeping your moves unexpected.

Law 18: Don't Build Fortresses to Protect Yourself— Isolation Is Dangerous
Engage with the world to stay informed and relevant.

Law 19: Know Who You're Dealing With—Do Not Offend the Wrong Person
Tailor your strategy based on understanding personalities and motivations.

Law 20: Do Not Commit to Anyone
Avoid overcommitting to others to maintain your flexibility and control.

Law— **16**

Use Absence to Increase Respect and Honor

"Absence diminishes little passions and increases great ones."

— François de La Rochefoucauld

Law 16: Use Absence to Increase Respect and Honor

This law suggests that sometimes, strategically withdrawing or making yourself less available can enhance your value and influence. Scarcity can increase others' appreciation for your presence and contributions.

The Power Behind the Principle

When people are always accessible, they may be taken for granted. By creating a sense of scarcity, you enhance others' perception of your value. The benefit is increased respect and honor, as well as potentially greater influence and allure.

Putting It to Use

- **Create a Sense of Scarcity**: Make yourself less available or present in certain situations, whether in person, in meetings, or on social media. By reducing your visibility, people will start to view you as more valuable and important, increasing the respect they have for you.
- **Take Strategic Breaks**: Withdraw from a situation or group for a short period to give others time to miss you. After taking time away, return with fresh energy and ideas, making your presence feel more impactful and appreciated.
- **Limit Your Availability**: Avoid always being readily available to respond to emails, texts, or calls. Instead, make others wait for your responses, so when you do respond, it feels more meaningful and significant.
- **Leave When the Moment Is Right**: When you're in a situation where your presence is being overused or underappreciated, step away before you wear out your welcome. Leave people wanting more of you by exiting at a point when your absence will create a sense of longing.
- **Create Mystery Around Your Actions**: Occasionally, remain silent or withhold information about your next move. By being unpredictable, you generate curiosity and intrigue, making people respect your judgment and value your opinion more when you do speak or act.
- **Be the „Elusive" Person**: Keep people guessing about your next steps or where you'll be. When people can't predict your actions, they'll start to

respect your autonomy and control. This unpredictability can enhance your power, making others more cautious in their interactions with you.

- **Limit Social Engagements**: Reduce your participation in social gatherings or public events. When you stop attending everything, people begin to recognize the value of your presence and are more eager to earn your attention and respect.
- **Cultivate a Reputation for Having a Busy Schedule**: Let it be known that you have a packed agenda and are always in demand. People will start to respect your time more and will prioritize you when they finally get a chance to engage with you.
- **Withdraw from Unimportant Battles**: Don't engage in every conflict or discussion. By stepping back from trivial matters, you preserve your energy and make your involvement in important issues seem more significant and worthy of attention.
- **Use Absence to Reaffirm Your Position**: If you're in a leadership role or trying to assert your authority, sometimes taking a step back or reducing your presence can remind others of your importance. They will realize that your involvement is essential and that their own power is diminished without you.

Recognizing When Others Use It

- They limit their availability or presence in certain settings.
- They occasionally withdraw from social or professional gatherings.
- They show up only at high-visibility moments.
- They avoid frequent communication, letting others reach out.
- They maintain a selective social or professional circle.
- They rarely share personal updates, maintaining mystery.
- They decline invitations or engagements strategically.
- They are selective about responding to requests.
- They create a sense of exclusivity around their time.
- They reappear after absences with renewed attention.

How to Neutralize Its Use

- Focus on your own goals without relying heavily on their presence.
- Build networks that do not depend on a single person's attention.
- Reach out to others when they are unavailable.

- Avoid idolizing their presence; maintain perspective.
- Document interactions and ensure continuity in their absence.
- Continue working proactively, focusing on objectives.
- Respect their absence without overanalyzing its purpose.
- Create value through your actions rather than seeking theirs.
- Stay focused on the team's success, with or without them.
- Recognize their tactic and avoid overcompensating for it.

Behaviors that Make You a Target

- **Being Always Available**: If you're constantly available, people will take your time and presence for granted. This behavior weakens your position and makes you less respected because your presence becomes expected rather than valued.
- **Overextending Yourself**: By trying to please everyone and be everywhere, you dilute your impact. This overextension leads people to see you as disposable, and they won't feel the need to value your time or contributions as much.
- **Lack of Boundaries**: If you fail to set boundaries and are always accessible to everyone, people will stop respecting your time and space. You become a resource they can tap into whenever they want, and this leads to exploitation.
- **Constantly Seeking Validation**: If you always crave attention and approval, you make yourself seem desperate for approval, which lowers your perceived value. People will start to manipulate this need by offering praise or validation when it suits their interests.
- **Failing to Maintain Mystery**: If you're an open book and people know exactly what you're up to all the time, you lose the element of intrigue. People will become complacent and stop respecting you, as they can predict your every move and reaction.
- **Never Taking a Break**: If you never step back or take time for yourself, people may begin to see you as a workhorse or tool to be used without regard for your well-being. Your constant availability makes you vulnerable to being exploited by those who see you as a resource to be consumed.
- **Getting Involved in Every Issue**: If you participate in every problem or argument, you become a constant fixture in people's lives. This lack of selectivity and discernment in where you invest your energy decreases your

perceived importance and invites people to take advantage of your time and efforts.

- **Being Over-Accessible on Social Media**: Constantly being available on social media or in digital communication makes you seem ubiquitous, which reduces your value. People won't see you as someone whose time or opinions are precious if they can always reach you instantly.
- **Being Overly Predictable**: If you always respond in the same way or are predictable in your actions, people will lose respect for you. Predictability makes you easy to manipulate, as others will know exactly how you will react or behave in certain situations.
- **Failing to Assert Yourself**: If you don't take time to make your presence felt or strategically assert yourself, you risk becoming invisible. Without setting boundaries and making yourself scarce at times, others won't respect your authority or value your input.

Law— **17**

Keep Others in Suspended Terror: Cultivate an Air of Unpredictability

"I am not afraid of an army of lions led by a sheep; I am afraid of an army of sheep led by a lion."

— Alexander the Great

Law 17: Keep Others in Suspended Terror: Cultivate an Air of Unpredictability

This law advises creating an air of unpredictability, making others unsure of your next move. This can deter rivals and increase your perceived power, as people are more cautious around you.

The Power Behind the Principle

When people cannot predict your actions, they are less likely to challenge you directly, and may instead work to stay on your good side. The benefit is greater control over your relationships, as well as increased influence through an aura of mystery.

Putting It to Use

- **Be Unpredictable in Your Actions**: Don't let people get comfortable predicting what you will do next. Change your patterns and behaviors frequently so that others can never quite figure you out. This will make them cautious and hesitant when dealing with you.
- **Keep Your Intentions and Plans Hidden**: Never fully reveal your intentions or strategies. Keep others guessing about what you're working on and what your next steps might be. When they can't anticipate your actions, they'll be less likely to make confident moves against you.
- **Incorporate Sudden Changes of Direction**: Occasionally change course or make sudden moves that leave people bewildered. If you're known for shifting strategies or taking unexpected actions, others will struggle to keep up with your plans, putting them at a disadvantage.
- **Remain Mysterious**: Limit the amount of personal information you reveal about yourself. Keep your thoughts, goals, and emotions to yourself, and only share what's necessary. By maintaining an aura of mystery, you make others wary and unsure of where you stand.
- **Create an Aura of Power and Control**: Cultivate an air of command and unpredictability by asserting your authority with confidence. When people aren't sure how you will react to situations or what you'll do next, they will respect your power and think twice before challenging you.

- **Be Inconsistent with Your Reactions**: Occasionally change your emotional responses or reactions to people's actions. By being unpredictable in your mood or decision-making, others won't know whether to expect praise, criticism, support, or rejection, forcing them to tread carefully.
- **Make Sudden Appearances and Disappearances**: Come and go as you please. Don't announce your arrival or departure, and don't let anyone get too comfortable with your presence. This keeps people alert, wondering when you'll reappear or take action.
- **Keep People Guessing About Your Loyalty**: Don't commit to alliances or friendships too readily. Make others uncertain about where your true loyalties lie. If people don't know if they can trust you completely, they'll be more cautious around you.
- **Use Silence to Your Advantage**: Occasionally withhold communication or go silent for a period. Not knowing where you stand or what you're thinking can make others uneasy. Silence can also make them eager to please you or do your bidding in order to gain favor.
- **Play With People's Expectations**: Create a reputation for surprising others—either by being generous one moment or ruthless the next. When you defy expectations, people can't rely on patterns, and they will act more cautiously, always wondering what you'll do next.

Recognizing When Others Use It

- They frequently change their approach or responses.
- They act unpredictably, making it hard to anticipate their actions.
- They withhold their intentions until the last minute.
- They shift strategies unexpectedly during discussions.
- They seem erratic in their reactions to similar situations.
- They avoid routines or regular commitments.
- They occasionally contradict their prior statements.
- They mix friendly gestures with abrupt decisions.
- They refrain from giving clear answers.
- They make surprising moves that catch others off guard.

How to Neutralize Its Use

- Stay calm and avoid overreacting to sudden changes.

- Focus on your goals rather than their unpredictability.
- Seek clarity and confirm decisions whenever possible.
- Document agreements or decisions to avoid confusion.
- Build a stable routine that isn't disrupted by others' actions.
- Set personal boundaries to manage erratic behaviors.
- Be adaptable and prepared for unexpected developments.
- Observe patterns over time to anticipate behaviors.
- Avoid letting their unpredictability deter your actions.
- Stay professional and consistent in your interactions.

Behaviors that Make You a Target

- **Being Predictable in Your Actions**: If you are always consistent in your behavior and decisions, others can easily figure out how you will react. This predictability makes you easier to control or manipulate because people will anticipate your responses.
- **Revealing Too Much About Your Intentions**: When you openly share your plans, goals, or strategies with others, they can anticipate what you'll do and adjust their actions accordingly. This transparency removes the element of surprise and makes you vulnerable to being outmaneuvered.
- **Always Following the Same Routine**: If your daily routine or responses are always the same, you become predictable. People can map out your actions, behaviors, and responses, which makes it easier for them to manipulate you or take advantage of your routine.
- **Over-committing to Alliances or Friendships**: If you pledge loyalty too easily or commit to people too quickly, they will see you as a fixed asset that's predictable and controllable. This limits your power and opens you up to manipulation from those who know you won't act unpredictably.
- **Being Transparent About Your Emotions**: If you make it easy for others to read your emotions or predict your mood, they can use this knowledge to manipulate you. By reacting consistently to certain triggers or emotions, you lose the ability to keep others in suspense about how you feel.
- **Always Reacting in the Same Way**: If you always respond to situations or challenges with the same behavior, people will come to expect this and will plan around it. A person who reacts predictably is much easier to manipulate or control than one who acts in surprising ways.

- **Being Overly Transparent or Open**: If you overshare your personal thoughts, weaknesses, or plans, people will know exactly what you're thinking and will be able to take advantage of you. They will use this information to exploit your vulnerabilities.
- **Lack of Boundaries**: If you make yourself constantly available or don't set limits on your time and energy, people will expect that you will always be there when needed. This expectation can be manipulated to take advantage of you, as they know your response will be predictable.
- **Allowing Others to Anticipate Your Actions**: If you always give people an idea of what you're going to do next or how you'll behave, they can plan accordingly and position themselves to counteract your moves. Being too open about your plans invites others to prepare for and control the outcome.
- **Avoiding Change or Sticking to One Strategy**: If you stick to one approach, whether it's a method of operation or a specific way of thinking, you become predictable and easy to manipulate. Those who understand your pattern will exploit it to gain the upper hand.

Law—**18**

Do Not Build Fortresses to Protect Yourself – Isolation is Dangerous

"If you want to go fast, go alone. If you want to go far, go together."

— *African Proverb*

Law 18: Do Not Build Fortresses to Protect Yourself – Isolation is Dangerous

This law cautions against isolating yourself for protection, as it can make you vulnerable to attacks and out of touch with valuable information. Staying connected keeps you informed and able to influence events.

The Power Behind the Principle

Isolation can lead to a lack of awareness and missed opportunities. By staying connected, you're more informed, adaptable, and resilient. The benefit is maintaining influence and avoiding the risks of being disconnected from important developments.

Putting It to Use

- **Stay Connected to Key People**: Regularly engage with influential people in your social and professional circles. Cultivate relationships with allies, friends, mentors, and even competitors. Staying connected ensures that you have access to valuable information and support when needed.
- **Monitor the Flow of Information**: Keep an eye on the social and political dynamics around you. Stay informed about changes, trends, and challenges within your industry, organization, or social group. You can't afford to be unaware of what's going on, as it may leave you vulnerable to shifts that could affect your power.
- **Create a Network of Allies**: Build a strong network of people who support and can help you when needed. By forming mutually beneficial relationships, you create a safety net of connections that will protect you from potential threats and provide assistance in times of need.
- **Engage in Public Activities**: Attend social events, meetings, and gatherings regularly to stay visible and engaged. Being active in the public sphere ensures that you remain connected and that your influence is felt, even if you're not the center of attention. It also allows you to observe others and adapt to their moves.
- **Share Your Plans with Trusted Confidants**: Avoid keeping your intentions completely secret. Share your plans, goals, and thoughts with trusted people

in your inner circle. This not only provides you with valuable feedback but also protects you from acting in isolation, where mistakes may go unnoticed.

- **Work Collaboratively**: Collaborate with others on projects and initiatives. Working together helps build trust, fosters creative thinking, and allows you to learn from others. Isolation makes you rely solely on your own judgment, which can be dangerous without external input.
- **Participate in Group Activities**: Get involved in group projects or teams where you can learn from others and stay engaged in the collective decision-making process. Isolating yourself from these group dynamics can cause you to miss key insights or opportunities for advancement.
- **Be Open to Feedback and Criticism**: Encourage others to give you feedback on your work, behavior, and decisions. Isolation breeds an echo chamber where only your own opinions matter. By remaining open to criticism, you stay grounded and aware of potential blind spots.
- **Diversify Your Social and Professional Circles**: Don't limit yourself to a small, closed group. Seek out new networks, attend conferences, join different organizations, and interact with people from various backgrounds. A diverse set of relationships helps you stay adaptable and ensures you're not trapped in a bubble where your perspective is limited.
- **Stay Engaged with New Ideas and Perspectives**: Expose yourself to new ways of thinking, whether through books, discussions, or seminars. Staying open to fresh ideas prevents stagnation and keeps you attuned to the latest trends and developments. By isolating yourself from outside influences, you risk falling behind or being blindsided by changes.

Recognizing When Others Use It

- They maintain open communication with multiple people.
- They avoid creating rigid boundaries or isolating themselves.
- They seek out diverse opinions and ideas.
- They participate in social gatherings or group discussions.
- They consistently network and build relationships.
- They remain involved in various projects or departments.
- They adapt their opinions based on new information.
- They avoid withdrawing when facing challenges.
- They keep a pulse on team morale and dynamics.
- They regularly engage with key stakeholders.

How to Neutralize Its Use

- Avoid isolating yourself in times of stress or pressure.
- Build a diverse network of contacts for support and feedback.
- Seek regular updates on important developments.
- Stay visible and approachable within your team.
- Encourage open discussions with colleagues.
- Avoid withdrawing from group interactions.
- Recognize the value of differing perspectives.
- Stay informed on team and industry trends.
- Foster collaborative relationships beyond your department.
- Be proactive in maintaining professional connections.

Behaviors that Make You a Target

- **Withdrawing from Social or Professional Life**: If you isolate yourself from others, people may begin to see you as weak or vulnerable. Isolation can create a sense of abandonment, making it easier for others to exploit you, as you won't have access to the support or information needed to defend yourself.
- **Cutting Off Relationships**: Severing ties with important connections, whether personal or professional, leaves you without the necessary alliances to safeguard your position. People who are cut off from key social or professional networks are easier to target, as they lack the protection of a broader community.
- **Not Engaging with Others' Opinions**: If you avoid listening to others or seeking advice, you risk becoming disconnected from reality. By neglecting other perspectives, you make yourself susceptible to manipulation, as your judgment becomes clouded and you lose awareness of potential threats.
- **Avoiding Conflict or Challenges**: If you retreat from difficult situations or avoid confrontations, you leave yourself open to others taking advantage of you. The act of isolating yourself to avoid confrontation may allow others to make moves in your absence, undermining your position.
- **Rejection of Teamwork**: If you consistently reject collaboration or team efforts, you isolate yourself from valuable contributions and support. Working alone can result in poor decisions due to a lack of diverse input, and

others may see you as easy to manipulate if you're not in the loop of shared knowledge.

- **Ignoring the Value of Feedback**: If you refuse to accept feedback or don't engage with others' opinions, you miss out on crucial information that could protect you from threats. Your own decisions become less informed, making you more susceptible to being outmaneuvered by others who have access to a broader perspective.
- **Becoming Complacent with Your Success**: If you become too confident and retreat from social or professional engagement because of past success, you risk becoming complacent. Without staying active and connected, you leave yourself vulnerable to challenges from rivals who are actively engaged.
- **Avoiding Networking or Socializing**: If you stop networking or avoid new relationships, you lose access to potential allies who could protect or support you. You may also miss opportunities for advancement or defense when others take advantage of your absence in social circles.
- **Limiting Your Access to Information**: If you isolate yourself from the flow of information by avoiding conversations or events where important information is shared, you become an easy target for others who are more informed. Isolation prevents you from learning about potential threats or opportunities before it's too late.
- **Refusing to Compromise or Adapt**: If you become rigid in your ways and refuse to adapt or listen to others, you risk creating an echo chamber where only your viewpoint exists. Being isolated in your thinking makes you less adaptable to changing circumstances, and others may exploit this by presenting you with solutions that are in their favor.

*Law—***19**

Know Who You're Dealing With – Do Not Offend the Wrong Person

---

"Treat people as if they were what they ought to be and you help them to become what they are capable of being."

— *Johann Wolfgang von Goethe*

Law 19: Know Who You're Dealing With – Do Not Offend the Wrong Person

This law advises being careful with whom you interact, as offending the wrong person can lead to unnecessary complications or retaliation. Understanding others' personalities helps you avoid conflicts with potentially powerful or vengeful individuals.

The Power Behind the Principle

Not everyone responds the same way to challenges, and some individuals may react more harshly to offenses. By being observant, you can navigate social dynamics and avoid triggering negative reactions. The benefit is preserving relationships, reducing risks, and avoiding potential pitfalls.

Putting It to Use

- **Conduct Thorough Research on People**: Before engaging with someone, take the time to understand their background, personality, values, and potential weaknesses. This will help you avoid unintentionally offending them and give you insight into how to approach the relationship.
- **Observe Their Reactions to Others**: Pay attention to how individuals behave toward others, especially when they feel slighted or disrespected. Observing their reactions to others' mistakes or offenses can help you gauge how they might respond to yours.
- **Understand the Power Dynamics**: Recognize who has influence and power in a given situation. Sometimes, the most dangerous people are not the ones who make the loudest claims, but the ones who have indirect power, like decision-makers or those with strategic connections. Know who controls what.
- **Respect Boundaries and Hierarchies**: Different people have different sensitivities and ideas about respect. Be mindful of social or professional hierarchies and avoid stepping on toes in areas where others may have more authority or emotional investment. Demonstrating proper respect avoids unnecessary conflict.

- **Gauge the Risk of Offending**: Before acting or speaking, consider the potential impact of your actions on the person you're dealing with. Ask yourself: Is this person in a position where they could retaliate, undermine, or harm me in some way? If so, be more cautious.
- **Be Diplomatic in Sensitive Situations**: If you need to address a conflict or sensitive issue, approach it diplomatically. Avoid direct confrontation or aggressive language, as it could provoke a stronger response from someone who values their reputation or position.
- **Adapt to Different Personalities**: People react differently to criticism, suggestions, or disagreements. Learn how to adapt your communication style to each individual. Some people may prefer indirect, subtle feedback, while others may want direct, blunt conversations.
- **Recognize Who Has Emotional Sensitivities**: Certain people may be more sensitive to criticism or perceived slights. Recognizing these emotional triggers can help you avoid making enemies inadvertently. This is especially important in personal and professional relationships where egos are often at play.
- **Stay Informed About Potential Threats**: Be aware of who is capable of harming you, whether directly or indirectly. A seemingly minor person in the office could have the ability to create a significant problem for you in the future, whether through gossip, alliances, or decision-making power.
- **Avoid Public Confrontations with Powerful People**: Avoid humiliating or embarrassing people in public, especially those who are in positions of influence. Public confrontation can breed resentment and trigger a desire for revenge, potentially ruining your reputation or position.

Recognizing When Others Use It

- They observe others carefully before engaging in conversations.
- They adapt their behavior based on who they are interacting with.
- They avoid challenging or confronting powerful individuals.
- They are cautious in their communication style around certain people.
- They sidestep sensitive topics in discussions.
- They seek to understand people's backgrounds and reputations.
- They maintain diplomacy and neutrality around influential figures.
- They take time to assess personalities before sharing opinions.
- They make calculated moves when addressing potential rivals.

- They subtly show respect toward those with strong personalities.

How to Neutralize Its Use

- Be aware of your own reputation and how it influences others' actions.
- Maintain professionalism and avoid unnecessarily provoking others.
- Avoid sensitive topics that could lead to misunderstandings.
- Clarify intentions if interactions seem tense.
- Build rapport gradually to avoid misinterpretation.
- Stay neutral on controversial issues to avoid conflicts.
- Observe how others respond to different personalities.
- Recognize when to hold back personal views.
- Respect others' boundaries and communication styles.
- Avoid taking offense if people seem cautious around you.

Behaviors that Make You a Target

- **Underestimating People's Power**: If you fail to recognize who holds influence or authority in a situation, you may inadvertently offend someone who has the power to harm your reputation, career, or goals. This can leave you vulnerable to manipulation by those with hidden power or influence.
- **Being Disrespectful to Hierarchical Figures**: Disrespecting someone in a higher position, whether a boss, leader, or authority figure, can lead to serious consequences. People who are higher up may have the means to retaliate against you in ways that can damage your career, reputation, or standing.
- **Ignoring Personal Boundaries**: If you fail to respect others' personal boundaries, whether emotional, professional, or physical, you risk offending them. People may begin to manipulate you by playing on your ignorance of their sensitivities or pushing you into uncomfortable situations.
- **Being Blunt Without Considering Others' Feelings**: Speaking directly without thinking about how it might affect others can make you appear rude or insensitive, potentially triggering a backlash. People might manipulate you into making more mistakes by exploiting your lack of social awareness.
- **Publicly Shaming People**: Humiliating or criticizing someone in public can create long-lasting resentment. People with the power to make your life difficult (whether through gossip, alliances, or direct authority) may turn your actions against you, leading to manipulation or retaliation.

- **Failing to Adapt to Different Personalities**: If you treat everyone the same, without adjusting your behavior to the nuances of each individual, you may unknowingly offend or alienate powerful people who may later manipulate situations to get back at you.

- **Ignoring People's Emotional Triggers**: If you don't take into account the emotional sensitivities of others—whether in the workplace or personal relationships—you can unwittingly create enemies. People may use your lack of awareness to manipulate you by exploiting your ignorance of their vulnerabilities.

- **Being Too Overconfident or Arrogant**: If you approach others with arrogance or an overinflated sense of superiority, you risk alienating individuals who may have the power to harm you. Others might use your arrogance as leverage to turn situations against you, manipulating you through your own ego.

- **Becoming Overly Familiar with Someone Powerful**: Acting too casually or presumptuously with someone who holds power can be a mistake. You may not realize that someone's seemingly friendly behavior masks a deeper resentment, and they could manipulate situations later to bring you down when you least expect it.

- **Failing to Read the Political Climate**: Ignoring the social or political dynamics at play can leave you blind to potential threats. Failing to recognize who's in control or who has the most influence in a given situation means you could inadvertently offend the wrong person or group, making you susceptible to manipulation.

Law—**20**

Do Not Commit to Anyone

"Sometimes the best way to solve your own problems is to help someone else."

— *Amir Gutfreund*

Law 20: Do Not Commit to Anyone

This law advises avoiding exclusive commitments, which may limit your options or tie you down to one party's interests. By remaining unattached, you keep others vying for your favor and maintain freedom in your decisions.

The Power Behind the Principle

Strong commitments can lead to dependence or loss of autonomy. Staying neutral allows you to adapt to changing situations and leverage multiple alliances. The benefit is increased flexibility, power, and influence, as people may compete to earn your commitment.

Putting It to Use

- **Maintain Strategic Independence**: Avoid forming strong allegiances or commitments that would tie you down. Cultivate an independent position where you're free to make decisions based on your own interests, not those of others.
- **Cultivate Multiple Alliances**: Build relationships with a wide variety of people, without fully committing to any one individual. This ensures that you have support from different directions, which prevents you from being fully dependent on a single person.
- **Avoid Over-Expressing Loyalty**: While it's important to show respect, avoid proclaiming undying loyalty to anyone. This can make you vulnerable to being used or manipulated, as people may expect that loyalty to be unconditional.
- **Keep Your Plans and Goals Flexible**: Stay adaptable and open to change. When you remain flexible, you avoid being stuck with one course of action or being manipulated into committing to a plan that may not be in your best interest.
- **Set Clear Boundaries**: Establish boundaries with those you interact with, particularly in terms of time, resources, and expectations. This helps you retain control and avoid being trapped in an agreement or situation you later regret.

- **Keep Your Emotions in Check**: Don't let emotional attachments cloud your judgment or decision-making. If you get too emotionally involved with someone, you become more susceptible to manipulation. Stay objective in your relationships and avoid letting emotions dictate your actions.
- **Be Cautious About Promises**: Be careful about making promises that tie you down to a person, group, or cause. Promises can create obligations, and once you're obligated, your freedom to act independently becomes limited.
- **Offer Support Without Full Commitment**: Help others and offer support when necessary, but avoid becoming fully committed to their projects or goals. This allows you to assist without being bound to their outcomes or having your interests tied to theirs.
- **Use Diplomacy and Tact**: If someone tries to pull you into their cause or align you with their goals, use diplomacy to politely decline or defer commitment. Make it clear that while you respect their position, you're not ready to fully commit.
- **Stay Free of Long-Term Obligations**: Avoid signing contracts, entering relationships, or making agreements that require long-term commitments. Keeping your options open allows you to pivot and adjust your course when circumstances change.

Recognizing When Others Use It

- They avoid aligning themselves fully with any group or person.
- They show interest in multiple perspectives without taking sides.
- They seem friendly with all parties without clear allegiances.
- They maintain a neutral stance in discussions and conflicts.
- They frequently change alliances based on circumstances.
- They appear hesitant to make long-term commitments.
- They avoid endorsing specific ideas or people strongly.
- They seem open to all options without confirming any.
- They encourage others to present their cases.
- They do not reciprocate overt loyalty, remaining independent.

How to Neutralize Its Use

- Avoid relying on their loyalty or commitment.
- Set clear boundaries and expectations in collaborative efforts.

- Assess their behavior over time to gauge reliability.
- Be prepared to pursue your goals independently.
- Do not invest too heavily in their support.
- Build additional alliances as a precaution.
- Encourage open communication about their intentions.
- Focus on your objectives without depending on their loyalty.
- Recognize when they avoid exclusive commitments.
- Respect their stance but maintain independence in your plans.

Behaviors that Make You a Target

- **Making Overly Strong Commitments**: If you commit yourself entirely to a person or cause, you become vulnerable to that person's influence. When you give your word without hesitation, others may take advantage of your loyalty and manipulate you into fulfilling obligations that don't serve your best interests.
- **Being Too Emotionally Invested**: Emotional attachment can cloud your judgment. If you allow your feelings to become deeply involved in a relationship or situation, others can exploit your emotions to manipulate or control you.
- **Always Being Available for Others**: If you're always available to meet the needs of others, it may be seen as a sign of full commitment. This dependence on others for validation or approval invites manipulation, as people may start to take advantage of your eagerness to please.
- **Letting Others Control Your Decisions**: If you allow others to dictate the terms of your relationships or professional commitments, you lose your independence and become an easy target for manipulation. When you're not in control of your own decisions, others can steer you in directions that benefit them.
- **Neglecting to Set Boundaries**: Failing to set clear boundaries—whether personal, professional, or emotional—leaves you open to exploitation. If you don't protect your time and resources, others can manipulate you into overcommitting or making unnecessary sacrifices.
- **Putting Others' Interests Before Your Own**: If you constantly prioritize others' goals over your own, you risk losing sight of your own interests. People may manipulate you by appealing to your sense of obligation or kindness, knowing that you're unlikely to refuse them.

- **Becoming Too Dependent on a Single Person**: Relying too heavily on one individual for advice, support, or guidance creates a dangerous dependency. This gives the other person significant power over your decisions and can make you vulnerable to their manipulation.
- **Over-promising or Over-delivering**: Promising too much can tie you down and create obligations that others can manipulate. By over-delivering on promises, you may set expectations that others will use to extract more from you, knowing you feel obligated to fulfill your commitments.
- **Aligning Yourself Publicly with Controversial Figures**: Committing to a person or group with a controversial or polarizing reputation can backfire, as it ties your reputation to theirs. People may manipulate you by leveraging that association to push their own agenda, knowing you're now tied to their image.
- **Being Too Loyal or Submissive**: Extreme loyalty can lead to submission, where you begin to lose your autonomy. If you continually defer to someone else, you make yourself an easy target for manipulation, as people will expect you to always put their needs before yours, and they will exploit this to their advantage.

PART V

Power in Action

Law 21: Play the Sucker to Catch a Sucker—Seem Dumber Than Your Mark

Disarm others by letting them underestimate you.

Law 22: Use the Surrender Tactic: Transform Weakness into Power

Turn setbacks into opportunities for future success..

Law 23: Concentrate Your Forces

Focus your energy where it matters most.

Law 24: Play the Perfect Courtier

Master the subtleties of influence and diplomacy.

Law 25: Re-Create Yourself

Redefine who you are to stay relevant and empowered.

*Law—***21**

Play a Sucker to Catch a Sucker – Seem Dumber Than Your Mark

"Sometimes it is better to pretend that you don't know anything."

— Paulo Coelho

Law 21: Play a Sucker to Catch a Sucker – Seem Dumber Than Your Mark

This law advises appearing less knowledgeable or capable than you truly are to encourage others to let down their guard. By underplaying your abilities, you can gather information or gain advantages that would be harder to obtain otherwise.

The Power Behind the Principle

When people underestimate you, they are more likely to reveal their intentions or make mistakes. Playing a "sucker" allows you to observe without appearing threatening. The benefit is greater insight, opportunities to learn, and the potential to outmaneuver others.

Putting It to Use

- **Feign Ignorance**: Act clueless or uninformed about key matters, even when you know exactly what's going on. This can make others believe they have the upper hand and allow them to reveal more than they should. People tend to lower their guard when they think they're dealing with someone less capable.
- **Ask Simple Questions**: By asking seemingly naive or simple questions, you can get people to explain things to you in detail. This often leads them to divulge more information than they intended, as they believe you lack the understanding to see through their actions or intentions.
- **Act Humble or Self-Deprecating**: Downplay your abilities or achievements to make others feel superior. When people think they are smarter or more capable than you, they may underestimate your potential and make strategic blunders that you can later exploit.
- **Pretend to Follow Others' Lead**: Act like you're simply going along with someone else's decisions, when in fact, you're quietly observing and gathering information. By making them think you're just a follower, you create an opportunity to control the narrative later.
- **Pretend to Lack Ambition**: Downplay your ambitions and goals, showing little interest in advancing or achieving too much. This can cause others to

view you as harmless or insignificant, which can prompt them to overlook you in critical situations.

- **Be Inattentive or Distracted**: Occasionally, give the impression that you are distracted, bored, or not fully engaged. People may think you're not paying attention and will let down their guard, allowing you to gather information or assess situations more freely.
- **Use False Modesty**: When discussing your skills or accomplishments, use excessive modesty. Instead of boasting about what you can do, understate your talents or achievements. This can trick others into underestimating your capabilities and give you the element of surprise.
- **Be Easily Influenced**: Pretend to be easily swayed by others' opinions or desires, showing that you lack strong will or independence. This can lead others to believe they can control or manipulate you, giving you the chance to quietly maneuver them into a more advantageous position for yourself.
- **Feign Vulnerability**: Present yourself as someone who is weak, easily overwhelmed, or unable to handle difficult situations. This can cause others to think you're an easy target, encouraging them to open up to you or let down their guard, while you remain alert and ready to act when the opportunity arises.
- **Play the Victim**: At times, act like you've been wronged or victimized by others. This can make you appear harmless and evoke sympathy, while simultaneously putting others in a position to overexplain themselves or offer solutions that you can manipulate to your advantage later.

Recognizing When Others Use It

- They downplay their skills or knowledge subtly.
- They act naïve or innocent in challenging situations.
- They ask basic questions to appear less informed.
- They listen more than they speak, especially around superiors.
- They pretend to misunderstand to encourage clarification.
- They seem overly agreeable or compliant.
- They defer to others despite apparent competence.
- They act surprised by compliments on their work.
- They avoid drawing attention to their achievements.
- They show selective understanding, being astute at times.

How to Neutralize Its Use

- Avoid underestimating their potential.
- Observe their behavior to see if they reveal hidden skills.
- Assess their past accomplishments for a more accurate view.
- Treat them with respect, regardless of their apparent knowledge.
- Recognize signs of feigned ignorance or compliance.
- Ask direct questions to clarify their expertise.
- Focus on facts over their perceived knowledge level.
- Maintain boundaries in case they have hidden motives.
- Do not let your guard down based on appearances.
- Stay objective and fair in evaluating their abilities.

Behaviors that Make You a Target

- **Overestimating Your Own Importance**: If you act like you're always in control or too capable, people may avoid revealing too much around you, thinking you're too sharp to fool. This can make them close off, leaving you with fewer opportunities to manipulate them or gain the information you need.
- **Being Overly Confident in Your Abilities**: If you're constantly showcasing your intelligence or talents, you risk making people wary of you. They may be less inclined to show their cards if they see you as a threat, thus preventing you from gaining valuable insight or gaining the upper hand.
- **Trying to Impress Others with Knowledge**: Constantly demonstrating your expertise or impressing people with your intelligence can make others take you seriously, potentially blocking your ability to get them to underestimate you. You may inadvertently position yourself as a target for competition or defense.
- **Being Rigid or Unyielding**: If you always insist on your views or act in a way that shows you're too opinionated or unbending, others will sense that you're not open to manipulation. Flexibility is key to making others believe they can lead you around, so being too set in your ways makes you more difficult to manipulate.
- **Overplaying Your Ambitions**: Talking too much about your plans for success and dominance can make you a target. People may see you as a threat or

try to use your ambition against you, making you a more obvious and less exploitable target for manipulation.

- **Acting Too Independently**: If you give the impression that you don't need help or guidance, people might feel threatened by your independence. They may be less inclined to reveal their intentions or make mistakes in your presence. Playing the „fool" allows you to move under the radar, so showing excessive self-sufficiency can backfire.

- **Taking Yourself Too Seriously**: If you're constantly serious, people will assume you are always on alert. When they know you're always „on," they won't let their guard down around you. This makes it harder to manipulate them because they won't reveal their plans, or they might even actively work to undermine your position.

- **Giving the Impression of Being Knowledgeable**: If you act like you have all the answers, people will stop trying to teach you things or provide you with critical information. By maintaining an aura of understanding, you limit your ability to catch others in mistakes or gain insight into their strategies.

- **Being Too Straightforward or Blunt**: If you are direct and assertive in your interactions, people may view you as an adversary or a potential threat. When others feel they cannot manipulate or control you, they will be less likely to reveal information or make themselves vulnerable to your influence.

- **Exposing Your Vulnerabilities Too Early**: If you open up too much about your weaknesses or desires too soon, people may try to take advantage of them. While playing a „sucker" involves feigning vulnerability, showing too much real vulnerability can cause others to either protect themselves from you or exploit you, preventing the opportunity for manipulation.

Law— **22**

Use the Surrender Tactic: Transform Weakness into Power

"Surrender to what is. Let go of what was. Have faith in what will be."

— *Sonia Ricotti*

Law 22: Use the Surrender Tactic: Transform Weakness into Power

When facing a stronger opponent, surrendering can allow you to bide your time and avoid immediate defeat. By yielding strategically, you can regain strength, observe your opponent, and eventually turn the tables.

The Power Behind the Principle

Surrendering can disarm an opponent, making them overconfident or less vigilant. It can also buy you time to regroup or strategize for future opportunities. The benefit is survival and the ability to seize control when the situation shifts in your favor.

Putting It to Use

- **Feign Weakness in the Face of Power**: If you are faced with an overwhelming adversary or force, pretend to surrender or concede defeat. By showing weakness, you create a situation where the other side relaxes, underestimates you, and lowers their guard, giving you a chance to regroup and strike later.
- **Appeal to Sympathy**: In situations where you're at a disadvantage, express vulnerability or humility to gain sympathy from others. This can transform people's perception of you, turning them into allies or at least people who are less likely to work against you.
- **Withdraw Temporarily to Gain Advantage**: Sometimes stepping back and retreating from a situation temporarily can allow you to reassess and plan your next move. This creates the illusion that you have been defeated or are not a threat, which can lead others to let their guard down.
- **Let Others Think They're Winning**: Allow others to feel that they are in control of the situation. By appearing submissive or compliant, you give them the false impression that they have achieved dominance, which will make them more vulnerable to a strategic counterattack later on.
- **Play the Long Game**: Surrendering or conceding in the short term allows you to build power and momentum for the future. Don't worry about winning

every battle—focus on positioning yourself for the final victory. Timing your surrender and recovery can be key to success.

- **Create False Weakness**: Pretend to lack the resources, skills, or willpower to accomplish a task or challenge. This will encourage others to make assumptions about your limits, leading them to act recklessly or overlook you, providing an opportunity for you to strike when they least expect it.

- **Appeal to the Ego of Others**: When surrendering or yielding, make sure the other party believes they have gained something valuable. Allowing them to feel superior or in control feeds their ego, which can make them more complacent and less likely to notice your real intentions.

- **Withdraw from Unnecessary Conflicts**: In situations where the cost of confrontation is too high, step back and avoid conflict. By doing so, you conserve your energy and resources, all while maintaining a neutral stance that leaves you the freedom to act later when the stakes are more in your favor.

- **Let Others Take Credit for Small Wins**: Sometimes surrendering on smaller points and allowing others to take credit for minor victories can pave the way for you to gain the upper hand on larger issues. This creates the impression that you're not a threat, while giving you time to plan and improve your position.

- **Use the „Feign Submission" Technique**: In the face of a difficult opponent, appear to submit fully to their wishes. This can make them complacent, thinking they have successfully dominated you. Once they believe you're no longer a threat, they may let down their guard, providing the perfect opportunity for a calculated comeback.

Recognizing When Others Use It

- They back down from conflicts without protest.
- They appear compliant or passive when facing opposition.
- They yield to authority but remain observant.
- They take on a supportive role rather than challenging leadership.
- They avoid confrontations, preferring patience.
- They comply with demands but maintain self-control.
- They wait for opportune moments to assert themselves.
- They offer concessions strategically.
- They show humility in front of stronger figures.

- They use surrender as a calculated move rather than defeat.

How to Neutralize Its Use

- Recognize that their compliance may be temporary.
- Avoid becoming overconfident due to their surrender.
- Observe their behavior for signs of future plans.
- Don't underestimate their potential influence.
- Consider their passive approach as strategic.
- Keep discussions open to prevent hidden agendas.
- Focus on long-term goals rather than short-term control.
- Set clear boundaries for their involvement.
- Monitor their role and contributions over time.
- Be prepared for them to assert themselves later.

Behaviors that Make You a Target

- **Being Too Eager to Fight or Win Every Battle**: If you always try to win every confrontation or resist giving up ground, you risk exhausting your resources and alienating potential allies. Others may perceive you as stubborn or overconfident, making it easier for them to manipulate you into unnecessary conflicts or overcommitments.
- **Appearing Too Confident in Your Position**: Overconfidence can make you appear unshakeable. This can prompt others to underestimate you, but it also risks making you too visible a target. If you're constantly asserting your power, others may recognize that you won't yield easily, and they may work around you rather than engage in direct manipulation.
- **Failing to Conceal Your Vulnerabilities**: Being open about your weaknesses or insecurities without a strategy to recover or turn them into a strength can lead to manipulation. If you don't transform your perceived weaknesses into a hidden advantage, others may exploit them to control or undermine you.
- **Being Overly Aggressive in Conflicts**: Constantly attacking or defending yourself without knowing when to retreat can make you appear like a threat, forcing others to take countermeasures. This aggressive behavior can drain your energy and resources, leaving you vulnerable to manipulation by those who understand the power of subtlety and patience.

- **Making Yourself Too Visible or Obvious**: If you make your intentions or desires too clear, people will be able to target your weaknesses directly. By making yourself an obvious figure of interest, you may end up in a situation where others exploit your position, knowing they can easily manipulate you.
- **Overcommitting to Causes or Alliances**: When you bind yourself too closely to a cause or group, you limit your flexibility and become predictable. If you tie yourself down too tightly, others will sense that they have leverage over you, making you more vulnerable to manipulation.
- **Fighting for Every Inch**: When you fight against every minor slight or challenge, it makes you appear inflexible and exhausting. This behavior can lead to you being overwhelmed by forces that could have been avoided or neutralized by adopting a more passive or yielding stance, waiting for a better opportunity.
- **Refusing to Back Down**: Insisting on never backing down can create an image of you as an unyielding opponent. While it can be seen as a show of strength, it may also cause you to alienate others who could have been potential allies, or lead to them manipulating you through indirect means rather than direct confrontation.
- **Being Overly Transparent About Your Desires**: If you are too open about what you want or where you stand, it can make you a predictable target for manipulation. People will be able to maneuver you into a corner where your options are limited, knowing exactly what you're after and how to take advantage of that knowledge.
- **Relying Too Much on Force**: Always opting for brute force or direct confrontation rather than using strategic surrender can cause others to recognize your predictability. If you rely on overpowering your enemies, you may miss the opportunity to subtly guide the situation in your favor by appearing weak at the right moments.

Law— **23**

Concentrate Your Forces

"He who is everywhere is nowhere."

— Seneca

Law 23: Concentrate Your Forces

This law advises focusing energy and resources on a single, strong goal. Spreading yourself too thin dilutes your impact, whereas concentrating power increases your influence and likelihood of success.

The Power Behind the Principle

Concentrated energy amplifies results, while scattered efforts are less effective. By directing efforts toward one objective, you maximize your impact. The benefit is increased strength, control, and the ability to accomplish significant achievements.

Putting It to Use

- **Focus on Your Most Important Goal**: Prioritize your most critical objectives and put your energy into achieving them. Identify the projects or relationships that offer the greatest potential for success and concentrate your time, resources, and efforts on them. Avoid diversions that don't contribute to your central aim.
- **Simplify Your Strategy**: Don't overcomplicate your approach. Streamline your efforts by narrowing your focus to just a few key actions that will create the most impact. Focus on the most effective ways to achieve your goals, rather than wasting energy on extraneous tasks.
- **Identify Your Key Allies**: Concentrate your resources on building and nurturing relationships with your most powerful or influential allies. By surrounding yourself with people who can help you achieve your goals, you enhance your ability to succeed. Don't waste time or energy trying to please everyone.
- **Leverage Your Strengths**: Identify your core strengths, talents, and resources, and focus on maximizing them. Instead of trying to improve your weaknesses, concentrate on the areas where you can excel, and apply all your energy toward developing and expanding those strengths.
- **Eliminate Distractions**: Remove activities, people, or commitments that do not align with your core objectives. By eliminating distractions, you free up your mental and emotional energy, allowing you to focus fully on what matters most.

- **Invest in High-Impact Opportunities**: When you do decide to invest time, money, or effort, do so in ways that have the potential to create the greatest return. Avoid spreading yourself too thin across multiple investments or ventures. Instead, pour your resources into opportunities that will maximize your impact.
- **Master One Skill at a Time**: Rather than trying to master multiple skills at once, dedicate yourself to mastering one at a time. This concentrated effort will yield better results than attempting to divide your focus. Once you've mastered one area, you can expand to others if necessary.
- **Avoid Overcommitting Yourself**: Resist the urge to take on too many projects or commitments. Focus your energy on the most important ones that align with your long-term goals. Spreading yourself too thin not only wastes time but also dilutes your power.
- **Streamline Your Resources**: Consolidate your resources—whether it's time, money, or people—into fewer, more focused channels. By concentrating resources, you can direct them more effectively and achieve a greater result with fewer inputs.
- **Embrace the Power of „No"**: Learn to say no to opportunities, people, or activities that are not directly related to your primary goals. Saying no allows you to conserve your energy and focus it where it counts. By turning down distractions, you stay in control of your time and resources.

Recognizing When Others Use It

- They focus intensely on one project or area of expertise.
- They avoid diversifying their commitments.
- They build specialized knowledge or skills.
- They direct resources toward a single objective.
- They dedicate time exclusively to a high-priority goal.
- They avoid distractions or side projects.
- They create a network around one specific purpose.
- They refuse offers that don't align with their main goal.
- They demonstrate deep expertise in a single domain.
- They prioritize one area of success over all else.

How to Neutralize Its Use

- Recognize the strengths of a focused approach.
- Avoid spreading yourself thin in response to their actions.
- Align your goals to match or complement their focus.
- Seek specialized knowledge to support your objectives.
- Focus on incremental achievements to balance efforts.
- Encourage diversified perspectives within your team.
- Build alliances around shared goals.
- Acknowledge the value of specialization but remain adaptable.
- Use their focus as a model to streamline your goals.
- Stay flexible to adapt to changes around the primary objective.

Behaviors that Make You a Target

- **Spread Yourself Too Thin**: When you try to juggle too many projects or relationships at once, you risk diluting your efforts. Others will see that you're distracted and might exploit your divided attention, pulling you in different directions or taking advantage of your inability to focus.
- **Fail to Prioritize**: If you don't identify your most important objectives and focus on them, others will impose their priorities on you. Without clear focus, you can be manipulated into giving attention to things that don't serve your true interests.
- **Overcommit Yourself**: Constantly saying yes to new opportunities or demands makes it hard to focus on your core objectives. People will begin to realize that you're overextended and may push you into commitments that dilute your power or drain your resources.
- **Ignore Your Core Strengths**: Failing to concentrate on your strengths means you may waste energy trying to excel in areas where you have little chance of succeeding. Others may take advantage of this weakness, leading you to squander resources in futile pursuits.
- **Waste Time on Low-Impact Activities**: Focusing on insignificant tasks or trying to please everyone can make you ineffective and vulnerable to manipulation. Others may recognize that you're spending too much time on the wrong things and might manipulate you into focusing on tasks that benefit them instead of you.

- **Become a Jack of All Trades**: Trying to master many different skills at once can lead to a lack of proficiency in any one area. People may take advantage of your inability to concentrate and become an easy target for those who are more focused and determined in a particular domain.
- **Lack of Boundaries**: If you allow yourself to be pulled into every situation and conversation, you'll soon find that others are dictating your focus. Without clear boundaries, your time and energy will be consumed by external demands, leaving you vulnerable to manipulation.
- **Fail to Say No**: If you're unable to turn down requests, people will begin to exploit your inability to focus and will push you into more commitments. When you say yes to everything, you give up control over your time, making you an easy target for manipulation.
- **Be Too Reactive to External Demands**: If you respond to every demand or crisis that arises, you'll lose sight of your long-term objectives. By constantly reacting to others, you make it easy for them to manipulate you, pulling you into their agendas instead of staying focused on your own.
- **Be Easily Distracted by New Opportunities**: If you're constantly jumping from one opportunity to another, you risk losing focus and failing to build momentum in any one area. Others may recognize your lack of focus and use it to manipulate you into chasing opportunities that benefit them, rather than staying on track with your own goals.

Law— **24**

Play the Perfect Courtier

"You don't have to blow out someone else's candle to make yours shine."

— Unknown

Law 24: Play the Perfect Courtier

This law suggests mastering the art of behaving like a perfect courtier, showing respect, tact, and charm to those in power. It involves subtly influencing others through politeness, strategic flattery, and avoiding overstepping boundaries.

The Power Behind the Principle

By playing the role of a respectful courtier, you gain favor and influence without directly challenging authority. The benefit is building alliances and goodwill that can serve your interests without causing resentment.

Putting It to Use

- **Master the Art of Flattery**: Give sincere and well-placed compliments that make people feel valued. However, ensure that these compliments align with the person's ego or desires. Flattery should be subtle and not overdone; too much can backfire, but a well-timed compliment can help you gain favor and trust.
- **Understand Power Dynamics**: Learn the power structure of any organization or social group and adjust your behavior accordingly. Position yourself in a way that shows respect for those with higher status, while subtly building alliances with those who can help you move up without drawing attention to your ambitions.
- **Be a Mirror to Those in Power**: Adapt your behavior to reflect the personalities, preferences, and values of the powerful individuals you wish to influence. By mirroring their actions and attitudes, you can make them feel more comfortable with you, which opens up opportunities for influence.
- **Know How to Make Others Feel Good About Themselves**: People in positions of power often have fragile egos. By making them feel admired and respected, you increase your chances of earning their trust and loyalty. Use subtle, tactful gestures or words to boost their self-esteem without appearing manipulative.
- **Be the Source of Gratitude**: Always be the one who offers help or support when someone in power is in need. By positioning yourself as indispensable,

you can make them feel grateful for your support. Gratitude leads to influence, and those in power are more likely to reward you for your loyalty.

- **Exercise Tact and Discretion**: Be careful what you say, especially in front of people who could potentially harm your reputation. The perfect courtier knows how to keep secrets, how to avoid unnecessary confrontation, and how to keep things running smoothly behind the scenes, creating a sense of trust and reliability.
- **Be Adaptable and Flexible**: The courtier can quickly adjust to changing circumstances and personalities. Whether the powerful figure is in a good mood or a bad mood, the courtier knows how to adapt their tone, energy, and attitude to fit the situation, creating a sense of harmony in the relationship.
- **Flatter Without Being Transparent**: Master the art of flattering someone while still remaining subtle. Make it seem as though you are paying them attention without overtly flattering them, allowing the powerful person to feel acknowledged without feeling manipulated.
- **Be a Quiet Listener**: Often, the best way to gain power over someone is to listen. The perfect courtier is a good listener who allows others to speak freely and express themselves. This builds trust and makes the powerful individual feel heard, creating a foundation for influence.
- **Never Outshine the Master**: Avoid showing off your abilities or outshining those above you, especially in public. The perfect courtier knows when to step back, praise others, and give credit where it's due. By doing so, you avoid arousing jealousy or insecurity in those in power, ensuring that they maintain a favorable view of you.

Recognizing When Others Use It

- They show deference and charm toward authority figures.
- They frequently offer compliments or praise.
- They avoid speaking over or contradicting powerful people.
- They practice subtle flattery.
- They avoid controversial opinions or confrontation.
- They are attentive to others' preferences and needs.
- They support others' ideas in public.
- They act diplomatically in all situations.
- They manage their image carefully.

- They position themselves close to power without seeming threatening.

How to Neutralize Its Use

- Maintain a professional distance without reciprocating excessive flattery.
- Acknowledge their support but focus on objectives.
- Observe their behavior for consistency.
- Set clear boundaries if interactions feel manipulative.
- Stay true to your values rather than mirroring their behavior.
- Recognize their approach but avoid being overly influenced.
- Keep interactions based on professional outcomes.
- Trust your judgment without overvaluing their praise.
- Engage in direct communication when needed.
- Be aware of their potential motives behind courtesies.

Behaviors that Make You a Target

- **Being Overly Direct or Confrontational**: If you're too direct or confrontational in your approach, you risk alienating those in positions of power. By being overly blunt or aggressive, you make it harder to play the role of the courtier, leaving you open to being manipulated or excluded from opportunities.
- **Failing to Adapt to Power Dynamics**: If you don't understand the power structures and fail to adjust your behavior accordingly, you will appear out of touch or out of sync with the key players. This could lead to your being sidelined, as others will recognize that you don't know how to navigate the political landscape.
- **Trying to Outshine the Powerful**: If you make it a habit of showing off your abilities, you risk making those in power feel threatened or insecure. Instead of gaining their favor, you may provoke jealousy or hostility, leaving yourself vulnerable to being undermined or ignored.
- **Being Overly Honest**: While honesty is generally a virtue, in power dynamics, being too blunt about your thoughts or intentions can make you appear tactless. The perfect courtier knows how to tell the truth without being abrasive, revealing only what is necessary, and never pushing the limits too far.

- **Being Too Eager to Please**: If you constantly seek to please others or always try to accommodate everyone's wishes, people may perceive you as insincere or manipulative. This can make you vulnerable to being used by those in power, who will exploit your desire to be liked or accepted.

- **Ignoring the Feelings of Those in Power**: If you disregard the emotions or egos of those in power, you risk losing their trust. The perfect courtier knows how to work with people's emotions—making them feel important, heard, and appreciated—without being overly obvious or manipulative.

- **Lack of Discretion or Tact**: The failure to exercise discretion can lead to revealing too much about others or about yourself, especially in sensitive situations. The perfect courtier keeps secrets, respects confidences, and avoids gossiping, all of which are qualities that make them trustworthy and influential.

- **Refusing to Adapt**: If you resist changing your behavior based on the needs and moods of those around you, you may appear inflexible and difficult to work with. Those in power are more likely to overlook you or even dismiss you if you don't show the ability to adapt.

- **Appearing Overly Independent or Ambitious**: If you constantly assert your independence or try to challenge the established hierarchy, you risk being perceived as a threat rather than an ally. This behavior will lead you to become isolated and possibly manipulated by those who feel threatened by your ambition.

- **Overestimating Your Worth or Influence**: If you believe that your influence or position is stronger than it actually is, you risk overstepping boundaries and alienating those in power. The courtier knows their place and plays it well, but when you overestimate your value, you become vulnerable to those who can expose or undermine your arrogance.

Law — **25**

Re-Create Yourself

"Life isn't about finding yourself. Life is about creating yourself."

— *George Bernard Shaw*

Law 25: Re-Create Yourself

This law encourages the conscious reinvention of oneself to adapt to different environments and maintain relevance. It involves shaping your image, behavior, and values according to your goals.

The Power Behind the Principle

By reinventing yourself, you stay adaptable, fresh, and prepared for different circumstances. This control over your image enhances your resilience and influence. The benefit is maintaining a dynamic presence, able to thrive in various settings.

Putting It to Use

- **Reinvent Your Image**: Periodically refresh your appearance, mannerisms, and even the way you speak or interact with others. A new image or persona can give you a fresh start and prevent people from pigeonholing you. This could be a change in style, adopting new interests, or even shifting your professional focus to something entirely different.
- **Adapt to New Situations**: Embrace change and adapt your behavior based on the environment you are in. Whether it's a new job, a new social circle, or a different political situation, being able to shift your persona to align with new contexts allows you to remain relevant and influential.
- **Stay Mysterious**: Don't reveal everything about yourself all at once. By keeping parts of your life or thoughts private, you create an aura of mystery that keeps others intrigued and cautious, which prevents them from forming a complete understanding of you and limits their ability to manipulate you.
- **Master Different Roles**: Learn to be versatile and play different roles depending on the situation. One day you may need to be the humble team player, and the next, you could be the bold visionary leader. Being able to switch between these roles allows you to navigate various social dynamics with ease.
- **Embrace New Skills and Knowledge**: Constantly improve yourself by learning new skills, knowledge, or expertise. Reinventing yourself isn't just about external changes; it's also about personal growth and broadening your capabilities, which enhances your value and makes you less predictable.

- **Challenge Expectations**: Don't let others define you by their assumptions or expectations. Challenge them by consistently defying what they believe you are capable of. Show them that you can be something more than they originally thought, keeping them on their toes and preventing them from taking you for granted.
- **Create a New Narrative**: Reframe your personal story or narrative. Whether it's how you describe your past experiences, your goals, or your vision for the future, the way you tell your story can shape others' perceptions of you. By creating a new narrative, you can align their view of you with your evolving goals.
- **Keep Evolving Your Social Circle**: Surround yourself with new people who bring different perspectives, challenges, and opportunities. As you evolve, so should your relationships. By continually introducing new influences into your life, you prevent yourself from becoming stagnant and predictable.
- **Learn to Reinvent in Small Steps**: Reinvention doesn't always have to be dramatic. It can be a gradual evolution of your character, appearance, and behaviors. Small, consistent changes in your approach and outlook allow you to remain dynamic while avoiding jarring shifts that could make you seem inauthentic.
- **Take Control of Your Public Image**: Be proactive in shaping how others see you. Use media, social platforms, or even word-of-mouth strategically to present a carefully curated version of yourself that fits your current goals. This control allows you to change your public persona and reduce the risk of being trapped in a fixed identity.

Recognizing When Others Use It

- They change their style, tone, or behavior to match situations.
- They often project a new image or personality.
- They align themselves with different trends.
- They adapt their speech to different audiences.
- They avoid sticking to a rigid identity.
- They remain open to changes in their approach.
- They project a well-crafted, deliberate persona.
- They seem to shift priorities based on new environments.
- They are comfortable with transformation.
- They distance themselves from previous roles or behaviors.

How to Neutralize Its Use

- Focus on authenticity in your interactions.
- Be mindful of their adaptability without overestimating them.
- Clarify goals to gauge their commitment.
- Stay consistent in your values and priorities.
- Recognize and adapt to their evolving tactics.
- Keep boundaries despite their changing approach.
- Stay objective about their image versus their actions.
- Recognize the influence of adaptability but maintain a steady stance.
- Reflect on your own principles without being swayed.
- Appreciate their flexibility while keeping your integrity intact.

Behaviors that Make You a Target

- **Sticking to One Identity**: If you allow others to define you by a single, static persona or role, you limit your ability to evolve and adapt. Others can use this fixed identity against you, manipulating you based on their perception of who you are and what you can do.
- **Being Predictable**: When people can easily predict your reactions, behavior, or choices, they will use that predictability against you. You risk being manipulated because others know exactly how to play you. Being dynamic and shifting your approach keeps others uncertain and wary of trying to control you.
- **Ignoring Personal Growth**: If you stagnate and stop learning or developing new skills, others will see you as someone who is no longer capable of evolving. This makes you vulnerable to being left behind or exploited, as people may no longer see you as a valuable or evolving asset.
- **Allowing Others to Dictate Your Role**: If you let others dictate how they perceive you or define your place in a group or organization, you give them the power to control your actions and limit your growth. This makes it easier for others to manipulate you, as they have a firm grasp on your boundaries and identity.
- **Revealing Too Much About Yourself**: Oversharing personal details or vulnerabilities can allow others to exploit your weaknesses. By being too transparent, you make it easy for others to anticipate your next move and use that knowledge to manipulate your behavior and decisions.

- **Focusing Only on Past Achievements**: If you continue to rely on your past successes or identity, you risk becoming irrelevant in the present. Others may use your past reputation to hold you back, and they might exploit your nostalgia or comfort with the past to manipulate your decisions and actions.
- **Resisting Change or Reinvention**: A refusal to change or reinvent yourself makes you more susceptible to being manipulated, as people will see you as rigid, unwilling to adapt, or stuck in your old ways. This makes you an easier target for those who know how to exploit this fixed mindset.
- **Lack of Self-Awareness**: If you don't actively manage your image and behavior, others can manipulate you by exploiting your lack of self-awareness. Without a clear sense of how you come across to others, you risk being taken advantage of or being influenced without realizing it.
- **Becoming Complacent in Your Success**: When you become too comfortable in your current position or identity, others may see it as an opportunity to manipulate you. Complacency often leads to stagnation, making you vulnerable to those who are actively reinventing themselves and staying ahead.
- **Being Too Attached to One Group or Person**: If you become too dependent on one group, person, or system for validation or success, you risk being manipulated by that group or individual. Your inability to diversify your influences and relationships makes it easier for others to control you.

Part VI

Long-Term Success and Legacy

Law 26: Keep Your Hands Clean
Maintain a spotless reputation while achieving your goals.

Law 27: Play on People's Need to Believe to Create a Cult-like Following
Inspire others to support and follow your vision.

Law 28: Enter Action with Boldness
Confidence can often determine the outcome.

Law 29: Plan All the Way to the End
Anticipate obstacles and stay focused on your goals.

Law 30: Make Your Accomplishments Seem Effortless
Hide the hard work and let others see only your brilliance.

Law— **26**

Keep Your Hands Clean

"The more you leave out, the more you highlight what you leave in."

— Henry Green

Law 26: Keep Your Hands Clean

This law advises avoiding direct involvement in messy or controversial actions to maintain a pristine reputation. Instead, delegate tasks that could damage your image, thus keeping your hands "clean."

The Power Behind the Principle

By keeping a clean image, you protect your reputation and avoid blame. Delegating controversial tasks reduces your risk of repercussions while allowing you to influence from behind the scenes. The benefit is an untarnished image and minimized liability.

Putting It to Use

- **Delegate Unpleasant Tasks**: Never directly engage in actions that could tarnish your reputation. Instead, delegate tasks that are morally or ethically questionable to others who are willing to take on the risk, all while remaining the image of the person who does no wrong.
- **Use Intermediaries**: If you need to influence or manipulate a situation, use third parties or intermediaries. By doing so, you can ensure that you remain untainted by the consequences, while the person or group you're using is left to handle the fallout.
- **Frame Others**: When something goes wrong, position others as responsible for the mistake or failure. Frame them in such a way that you appear blameless, even though you may have orchestrated events from behind the scenes.
- **Create a Public Persona of Integrity**: Maintain a public image of someone who is above reproach—someone who is constantly acting in the public's best interest. This allows you to deflect any accusations of impropriety and protects you from guilt by association.
- **Keep Your Involvement Hidden**: If you need to be involved in a morally dubious situation, make sure that your involvement is kept secret. Work behind the scenes, making sure that others take the fall, while you maintain the appearance of innocence.
- **Use Legal or Ethical Loopholes**: When faced with a situation that could tarnish your reputation, use legal or ethical loopholes to avoid blame. By

bending the rules just enough without breaking them, you can keep your hands clean while getting the results you desire.

- **Create Distance Between Yourself and Negative Actions**: If negative actions are being carried out by your subordinates or allies, ensure that there is a clear distance between you and those actions. For instance, when things go wrong, publicly dissociate yourself from those who made the mistakes, emphasizing that you were not involved in those decisions.
- **Use Scapegoats**: When you need to make a tough decision or implement harsh actions, use scapegoats to take the blame. Find someone who is expendable and pin the responsibility on them, while keeping your hands clean and your image intact.
- **Manipulate Public Perception**: Control the narrative by manipulating public perception. If something negative occurs, spin it in such a way that it looks like someone else is at fault, or that you were an unwilling participant. This can be done through controlled leaks, framing, or public relations strategies.
- **Avoid Direct Confrontation**: Instead of engaging in a direct confrontation or taking part in a morally questionable decision yourself, influence the outcome from the sidelines. By maintaining a neutral stance, you can appear to be innocent, even if you are the one pulling the strings behind the scenes.

Recognizing When Others Use It

- They delegate controversial tasks to others.
- They rarely take responsibility for conflicts.
- They maintain a calm, professional demeanor.
- They avoid discussions of errors or issues.
- They subtly distance themselves from controversies.
- They appear impartial or above disputes.
- They frequently credit others for handling delicate matters.
- They shift attention away from their involvement.
- They emphasize their fairness and neutrality.
- They praise others' work in sensitive situations.

How to Neutralize Its Use

- Recognize when tasks are delegated unfairly.
- Clarify responsibilities and roles before starting projects.

- Avoid taking sole responsibility for controversial tasks.
- Document your contributions and actions.
- Be cautious about taking on sensitive assignments.
- Ensure transparency when decisions are made.
- Observe how they respond to issues and challenges.
- Stay neutral and don't shoulder others' mistakes.
- Hold them accountable if they avoid responsibility.
- Protect your reputation by setting clear boundaries.

Behaviors that Make You a Target

- **Taking Responsibility for Every Situation**: If you are the one always volunteering to handle difficult, morally gray, or controversial situations, you are putting yourself at risk of being seen as complicit. This opens you up to manipulation, as people may use your willingness to take responsibility against you.
- **Being Too Transparent with Your Involvement**: If you are too open about your involvement in questionable activities or decisions, you make it easy for others to target you. People will use your transparency to implicate you in things that can harm your reputation or put you at a disadvantage.
- **Failing to Use a Buffer**: If you don't use intermediaries or third parties when dealing with tough situations, you make yourself vulnerable to being directly associated with the fallout. Without a buffer, others will see you as the one pulling the strings, making you an easy target for blame or manipulation.
- **Acting Impulsively Without a Plan**: If you act impulsively and without foresight, you risk being associated with negative outcomes or losing control of a situation. Others may exploit your lack of strategy to manipulate you into a position where you're held accountable for something you didn't want.
- **Being Too Trusting or Loyal to the Wrong People**: If you trust or become loyal to individuals who are willing to take unethical actions, you may find yourself dragged into a situation where you are compromised. Manipulative individuals can exploit your loyalty by involving you in their schemes, putting you at risk of becoming collateral damage.
- **Ignoring the Consequences of Your Actions**: If you fail to consider the long-term consequences of your actions, you invite others to manipulate the situation to their advantage. Inattention to the fallout could leave you

vulnerable to blame when things go wrong, especially if others start to point fingers.

- **Becoming Emotionally Involved in Decisions**: When you allow your emotions to dictate your decisions, you become easier to manipulate. Emotionally driven decisions can cloud your judgment, making you more susceptible to being swayed or misled by those who understand how to play on your feelings.
- **Letting Others Know You're Not Above Reproach**: If you make it clear that you have no moral boundaries or that you're willing to get your hands dirty, people will have less reason to protect you and will be more likely to manipulate you. When you show a lack of discretion, others will use that against you.
- **Taking On Too Much Personal Risk**: If you take on excessive personal risk in a situation—whether in business, social, or political environments—you make yourself a target for exploitation. Being seen as the one willing to take the fall leaves you exposed to being manipulated by others who prefer to remain safely in the background.
- **Ignoring Your Reputation**: When you don't actively manage your reputation and protect your image, you become vulnerable to manipulation. People who are aware of your flaws or willingness to bend the rules can manipulate you into compromising your principles or taking on actions that will harm your reputation.

Law— **27**

Play on People's Need to Believe to Create a Cult-like Following

"The crowd will follow a leader who tells them what they want to hear."

— *Napoleon Bonaparte*

Law 27: Play on People's Need to Believe to Create a Cult-like Following

This law suggests appealing to others' desire for purpose or belonging, positioning yourself as a source of guidance. By fulfilling their need to believe, you can inspire loyalty and influence.

The Power Behind the Principle

People often seek meaning and direction, and by positioning yourself as a leader or visionary, you can cultivate a loyal following. The benefit is strong influence and loyalty, as followers are less likely to question or challenge you.

Putting It to Use

- **Create a Powerful Vision**: Develop a bold, captivating vision or mission that resonates with people's desires and fears. Make your vision bigger than life and create a sense of destiny or purpose. The more people feel they are part of something significant, the more likely they are to follow you loyally.
- **Build a Charismatic Persona**: Cultivate a charismatic and magnetic personality. People are naturally drawn to those who appear confident, visionary, and larger-than-life. Develop your personal brand by being seen as someone who has all the answers or possesses rare, invaluable knowledge.
- **Offer a Sense of Belonging**: Make people feel that by following you, they are part of an exclusive group with a special bond. Create a sense of community where followers feel united by shared values or a common purpose. This can be a physical community (like a team or organization) or a more abstract one (like an ideological or spiritual movement).
- **Create a Myth Around Your Identity**: Build a mythology around yourself, portraying yourself as a figure of extraordinary power, wisdom, or destiny. Make your background, story, or personal journey seem epic or mysterious. The more myth-like your persona, the more others will be inclined to believe in you.
- **Use Symbols and Rituals**: Create symbols, rituals, or practices that followers can engage with. These serve to solidify their commitment to you and your movement. Whether it's a special handshake, mantra, or ceremonial practice,

these rituals will reinforce the sense of belonging and the seriousness of their commitment.

- **Play on People's Deepest Needs**: Tap into the deep psychological needs of your followers, such as their need for certainty, belonging, or transcendence. Offer them solutions to their problems—whether existential, emotional, or social—that make them feel your teachings or vision are the only way to achieve fulfillment.
- **Be a Source of Mystique**: Maintain an aura of mystery around yourself. Don't reveal too much about your personal life or motivations. By keeping certain aspects of yourself enigmatic, you make people more intrigued, allowing you to manipulate their curiosity and deepen their attachment to you.
- **Use Language That Inspires Devotion**: Speak in a way that stirs emotion and loyalty. Use words that convey purpose, strength, and a sense of higher calling. When you speak to your followers, your words should feel like they are imparting wisdom, offering truth, or leading them to a better world.
- **Create a Sense of Urgency**: Instill a sense of urgency or crisis in your followers. Make them believe that the world is in dire straits and that only by following you can they survive, thrive, or become part of something revolutionary. People are more likely to follow when they feel there is no time to waste.
- **Offer a Solution to Their Struggles**: Be the answer to people's struggles, whether they are personal, professional, or societal. Offer clarity where there was confusion, comfort where there was distress, and purpose where there was aimlessness. By providing a clear solution, you can capture people's trust and make them believe in your leadership.

Recognizing When Others Use It

- They emphasize a strong vision or mission.
- They use charismatic language to inspire.
- They frequently speak about values or beliefs.
- They create a sense of exclusivity around their ideas.
- They encourage followers to adopt a unified mindset.
- They foster a sense of community around their goals.
- They discourage dissent or opposing views.
- They present themselves as a source of guidance.
- They focus on emotional appeal in communication.

- They position their ideas as transformative or unique.

How to Neutralize Its Use

- Maintain a balanced perspective on their ideas.
- Question decisions and directions that lack evidence.
- Avoid blind commitment without personal analysis.
- Set boundaries between loyalty and critical thinking.
- Recognize the power of emotional appeal and stay objective.
- Stay informed and think independently.
- Avoid groupthink by seeking diverse viewpoints.
- Focus on facts and results over rhetoric.
- Assess their motives and long-term intentions.
- Encourage open dialogue within the group.

Behaviors that Make You a Target

- **Desperation for Leadership**: If you are desperate for guidance or leadership and constantly seek someone to follow, you are more susceptible to being manipulated. Individuals who see you as needing them can take advantage of this by positioning themselves as the source of salvation, exploiting your emotional vulnerability.
- **Blind Trust in Authority Figures**: If you place too much trust in charismatic or authoritative figures without critically evaluating their motives, you open yourself up to manipulation. A lack of skepticism makes it easy for someone to manipulate your beliefs or behavior for their own gain.
- **Looking for a Cause to Attach to**: If you're constantly seeking a cause, group, or movement to latch onto because you lack a sense of purpose or direction in your life, you are a prime target for individuals who want to create a cult-like following. Your desire to belong will make you susceptible to leaders who promise meaning and direction.
- **Over-Identification with a Group or Leader**: If you start to define yourself entirely through the group or leader you follow, you risk losing your individuality and critical thinking ability. Cult-like leaders thrive on this kind of devotion, as they can easily manipulate you when you no longer have an independent sense of self.
- **Disregard for Personal Boundaries**: If you constantly allow others to cross your personal boundaries or make you feel compelled to give up your

autonomy for the group, you are being manipulated. Cult-like followers often feel that they must surrender their personal identity to the cause, leaving them open to exploitation.

- **Constant Need for Validation**: If you rely on constant validation from others, especially from those in positions of power, you make yourself vulnerable to manipulation. Cult-like leaders use this need to build dependency and reinforce loyalty, making it difficult for you to see the manipulation at play.
- **Ignoring Red Flags or Unhealthy Dynamics**: If you ignore warning signs of unhealthy dynamics, such as manipulation, exploitation, or coercion, you are more likely to fall prey to a cult-like environment. Leaders often create situations where you feel compelled to ignore your own instincts to maintain the facade of unity or loyalty.
- **Desire for a Quick Fix**: If you are looking for a fast solution to your problems or life struggles, you may be more susceptible to charismatic figures who promise easy answers. Manipulative leaders often prey on those in search of simple solutions, offering them a false sense of certainty.
- **Being Easily Influenced by Emotional Appeals**: If you are easily swayed by emotional appeals or persuasive rhetoric without considering the facts or logic, you open yourself to manipulation. Cult leaders often rely on emotional persuasion to create intense loyalty, making it difficult to question their motives or actions.
- **Relinquishing Personal Responsibility**: If you regularly abdicate your responsibility for your own decisions and look to others to lead you, you give up your power and control. This makes it easier for others to manipulate you into following them blindly, as you have given up the ability to think critically or independently.

Law— **28**

Enter Action with Boldness

"Fortune favors the bold."

— Virgil

Law 28: Enter Action with Boldness

This law advises that when you take action, you should do so decisively and with confidence. Bold moves can intimidate opponents and prevent them from interfering.

The Power Behind the Principle

Boldness breeds authority, while hesitation invites others to question or challenge you. Taking decisive action gives you control over situations and encourages others to follow or respect you. The benefit is that you project strength, minimize doubt, and create momentum.

Putting It to Use

- **Decide Quickly, Act Immediately**: When presented with an opportunity or decision, avoid overthinking or second-guessing. Make your decision swiftly and act on it without delay. Boldness in execution is often more powerful than waiting for the "perfect" moment.
- **Project Confidence in Every Action**: Whether it's a small decision or a major move, ensure you carry yourself with confidence. Speak clearly, walk with purpose, and exhibit physical presence. Confidence is contagious, and people will be more likely to follow you if you display certainty.
- **Make Decisive and Assertive Moves**: In any situation, make it clear that you are in control. Even if you have doubts, taking swift and assertive action shows leadership. Hesitation only gives room for others to question your ability or authority.
- **Commit Fully to Your Decisions**: Once you've made a decision, don't second-guess or waver. Fully commit to it, even if you are uncertain about the outcome. Indecision can make you appear weak, whereas full commitment will often inspire confidence in others.
- **Embrace Risks**: Boldness often involves taking calculated risks. If the reward is worth the risk, don't be afraid to make bold choices even if they seem dangerous or unconventional. Playing it safe can often lead to missed opportunities.
- **Appear Unshakable**: In moments of doubt or crisis, maintain an unshakable stance. Whether facing criticism, resistance, or uncertainty, your ability to

appear calm, composed, and in control will make others believe that you know exactly what you're doing.

- **Take the Initiative**: Never wait for others to take the lead or decide the course of action. When you see an opportunity or need, take it. The person who steps forward with a clear vision and path is often seen as the natural leader.
- **Use Strong Body Language**: Boldness is not just a mental state—it must be reflected physically. Use strong, purposeful body language: stand tall, make eye contact, and speak with conviction. Your physical presence reinforces the confidence you want to project.
- **Speak with Authority**: When you speak, do so as if you are the expert, even if you're not. People are more likely to trust someone who speaks with authority, and boldness can lend weight to your words. Speak clearly, avoid hesitations, and stand by your statements.
- **Set a Clear Direction**: When leading others, provide a clear vision and path for success. Boldness isn't just about taking action; it's about taking action in a way that others can follow. Set goals and priorities with confidence, and ensure everyone understands the direction you're heading in.

Recognizing When Others Use It

- They act confidently even in uncertain situations.
- They make decisive statements or decisions.
- They avoid hesitation or second-guessing.
- They take initiative, often in high-stakes moments.
- They demonstrate an "all-in" attitude.
- They make others feel empowered by their certainty.
- They avoid showing vulnerability in their choices.
- They focus on clear goals and objectives.
- They lead by example through actions, not words.
- They project a sense of inevitability in their plans.

How to Neutralize Its Use

- Question decisions if they seem impulsive.
- Assess the risks and benefits of their actions.
- Remain composed and avoid being intimidated.

- Gather additional information before following.
- Stay cautious and avoid acting without clarity.
- Seek alternatives or backup plans if needed.
- Verify their goals and intentions.
- Focus on logic over bold impressions.
- Balance confidence with prudence.
- Avoid being rushed into commitments.

Behaviors that Make You a Target

- **Hesitating or Showing Uncertainty**: If you hesitate or appear uncertain when making decisions or taking action, you invite doubt from others. This weakens your position and makes you vulnerable to manipulation. Others will see you as indecisive and may attempt to push their agenda.
- **Overthinking and Overanalyzing**: Constantly overanalyzing a situation without taking action shows a lack of boldness. This behavior invites manipulation because it reveals that you are not capable of making firm decisions, making it easier for others to sway you.
- **Being Easily Influenced by Others' Opinions**: If you frequently seek validation or second opinions from others, it undermines your own authority and creates the appearance of weakness. Manipulative individuals will exploit this behavior by influencing your decisions or actions based on their own interests.
- **Not Following Through on Decisions**: If you make decisions but fail to act on them or change your mind frequently, you signal a lack of conviction. This creates an opening for others to take advantage of your indecision and manipulate the situation to their benefit.
- **Acting Out of Fear**: If you make decisions based on fear—whether of failure, rejection, or consequences—you will show vulnerability. Manipulative people will prey on your fears and use them to push you into actions that are not in your best interest.
- **Lack of Self-Confidence**: If you constantly doubt yourself or your abilities, it will be obvious to those around you. Manipulative individuals can detect self-doubt and use it to exploit you. Confidence is a shield, and without it, you become an easy target.
- **Seeking Consensus Instead of Taking Action**: When you always seek the approval of others before taking any action, you give up control. A

manipulator can exploit your need for consensus and use your indecision to steer you toward their own desires.

- **Being Too Cautious or Risk-Averse**: If you are overly cautious and avoid risks altogether, you signal that you're not willing to step outside your comfort zone. This can make you appear weak or unambitious, opening you up to being manipulated by those willing to take risks on your behalf.
- **Deferring Responsibility to Others**: If you consistently defer responsibility to others and fail to take ownership of your actions or decisions, you come across as weak and indecisive. This behavior leaves you open to manipulation, as others will take advantage of your unwillingness to lead.
- **Failing to Set Boundaries**: If you fail to assert your own boundaries and let others dictate the terms of your involvement or decisions, you invite manipulation. Without clear limits, others can easily push you into actions that serve their interests, not yours.

Law— **29**

Plan All the Way to the End

"By failing to prepare, you are preparing to fail."

— Benjamin Franklin

Law 29: Plan All the Way to the End

This law advises anticipating the outcome of your actions by planning all steps thoroughly. By visualizing the end, you minimize surprises and maintain control over the outcome.

The Power Behind the Principle

When you plan meticulously, you're less likely to be caught off guard by unforeseen obstacles. This foresight allows you to adjust proactively and complete your goals smoothly. The benefit is greater control, fewer setbacks, and a clear path to success.

Putting It to Use

- **Set Clear Long-Term Goals**: Begin by defining your ultimate objective. Whether it's a personal goal or a larger strategic ambition, ensure you have a clear vision of what you want to achieve in the long term. This long-term vision will guide all your actions and decisions.
- **Visualize the Entire Process**: Don't just focus on the immediate next step. Picture the entire sequence of events, from your starting point to your final outcome. Anticipate every challenge, opportunity, and potential setback that could arise along the way. This visualization helps you to remain prepared for unexpected situations.
- **Break Down the Big Picture into Smaller Milestones**: Break down your long-term goals into smaller, manageable tasks or milestones. This keeps you on track and provides measurable progress points. It also allows you to adjust your plans if needed while still keeping your eye on the ultimate end goal.
- **Account for Possible Obstacles**: Think through the potential obstacles or resistance you might face at every stage of the process. Plan strategies to overcome these hurdles in advance. The more proactive you are, the less likely you will be caught off guard.
- **Factor in the Reactions of Others**: Anticipate how others might react to your actions at every stage. Consider their goals, fears, and motivations, and plan accordingly. Understanding others' likely behavior allows you to navigate their actions and remain in control of the situation.
- **Have Contingency Plans**: No plan is foolproof. Always have backup plans in place in case things don't go as expected. Having several options available

ensures that you are never caught without a solution, and it gives you the flexibility to adapt without losing momentum.

- **Time Your Actions with Precision**: Timing is critical in any plan. Understand when to act, when to wait, and when to make your move. Being able to control the timing of your actions can turn the tide in your favor, especially when the element of surprise is on your side.
- **Look for Patterns and Predict Trends**: Use past experiences, observations, and research to anticipate patterns in behavior, market dynamics, or even social trends. Being able to predict what is likely to happen next gives you an advantage in maintaining control over a situation.
- **Consider the Long-Term Consequences of Your Actions**: Be aware of how your actions today might affect your future power and influence. Every decision you make should be in line with your long-term objectives, so you can avoid short-term wins that could jeopardize your lasting success.
- **Keep Your Plan Flexible**: While it's important to have a long-term plan, also be flexible and adaptable. The ability to adjust your strategy based on new information or changing circumstances will help you stay ahead of competitors or unforeseen challenges, all while staying on course to your end goal.

Recognizing When Others Use It

- They break down their goals into specific steps.
- They anticipate possible challenges and solutions.
- They avoid impulsive decisions in complex matters.
- They ask questions about long-term effects.
- They prepare backup plans and contingencies.
- They focus on the big picture and the end result.
- They are disciplined in following through on plans.
- They seek advice to fill knowledge gaps.
- They regularly evaluate their progress.
- They avoid commitments that lack clear outcomes.

How to Neutralize Its Use

- Ensure clear roles and responsibilities in their plans.
- Monitor the consistency between words and actions.

- Avoid assuming they've accounted for all variables.
- Assess if the plan aligns with shared goals.
- Prepare your own contingencies if impacted.
- Seek clarity on any vague aspects of their plan.
- Be cautious of overconfidence in their foresight.
- Encourage adaptable plans if circumstances change.
- Consider alternative solutions alongside their approach.
- Keep communication open for ongoing input.

Behaviors that Make You a Target

- **Lack of Long-Term Vision**: If you only focus on the short-term or immediate rewards, you leave yourself vulnerable to being manipulated. Without a clear end goal, others can steer you off course or take advantage of your lack of direction.
- **Impatience for Results**: If you are impatient and eager for quick results, you may make hasty decisions without considering the long-term consequences. This impatience opens the door for others to exploit your desire for fast gratification by pushing you toward poor decisions.
- **Relying on Reactive Thinking**: If you only react to situations as they occur and fail to anticipate future outcomes, you expose yourself to manipulation. Those who can plan ahead will be in a stronger position to guide you toward decisions that align with their interests, not yours.
- **Ignoring Potential Challenges**: If you fail to consider or prepare for possible obstacles, you are likely to encounter surprises that disrupt your progress. A lack of foresight makes it easier for others to take advantage of your unpreparedness, leading you down a path of failure.
- **Failing to Anticipate Others' Moves**: If you don't consider how others will react to your actions, you may end up blindsided. Manipulators thrive on unpredictability, and if you don't plan all the way to the end, you might fall victim to their calculated responses.
- **Exposing Your Uncertainty**: If you show doubt about your long-term plans or goals, others can exploit your uncertainty. People with more clarity or conviction will use your hesitation against you to shift the direction of your decisions.
- **Overlooking the Bigger Picture**: If you focus on small wins or minor details at the expense of the broader strategy, you make yourself susceptible to

manipulation. Manipulators can distract you with trivial matters, keeping you from seeing how their actions affect your overall objective.

- **Being Easily Influenced by Immediate Circumstances**: If you allow the current circumstances to dictate your actions without considering how they fit into your long-term goals, you become vulnerable to manipulation. A manipulative individual can take advantage of this shortsightedness to push you off course.
- **Giving Up Control**: If you relinquish control of the planning or decision-making process, you open the door for others to steer the plan in their favor. Those who can control the planning process will manipulate the outcome to align with their objectives rather than yours.
- **Lack of Preparedness for Setbacks**: If you do not plan for setbacks or failure, you are likely to be caught off guard and susceptible to others' influence when things go wrong. Manipulators can prey on your panic or desperation when things don't go according to plan, leading you to make decisions you wouldn't otherwise consider.

*Law—***30**

Make Your Accomplishments Seem Effortless

"The height of cultivation always runs to simplicity."

— Bruce Lee

Law 30: Make Your Accomplishments Seem Effortless

This law advises presenting your successes as if they required little effort, even when they involved hard work. By concealing the effort, you project skill, competence, and control, enhancing your reputation.

The Power Behind the Principle

People admire talent that appears innate rather than laborious. Presenting accomplishments as effortless prevents others from seeing your struggles and vulnerabilities. The benefit is increased respect, mystique, and authority.

Putting It to Use

- **Master Your Craft in Private**: Put in the hours of practice, learning, and trial behind closed doors. When you perform, whether in a professional or social setting, make it look as if the skill or accomplishment came easily. This allows you to maintain control over the image of your effortless success.
- **Don't Over-Explain Your Process**: When sharing your accomplishments, avoid going into too much detail about the effort or struggles involved. Focus instead on the results, and make it seem like your success was natural and inevitable. Keeping the hard work behind the scenes adds to the mystique.
- **Downplay the Struggles**: If people inquire about the challenges you faced, downplay them or dismiss them as minor obstacles. Focus on the ease of your victory rather than the battles. This reinforces the image of effortless success.
- **Maintain Grace Under Pressure**: When facing difficulties, show calmness and poise. Don't let people see you sweat or get flustered. The more composed you appear, the more others will believe that achieving your goals comes naturally, even if you're experiencing pressure.
- **Control Your Image and Narrative**: Be deliberate in how you present your successes to the world. Choose the moments when you reveal them and ensure you highlight the effortless nature of your achievements. By controlling the narrative, you shape how others perceive your accomplishments.
- **Use Subtlety to Convey Power**: Instead of flaunting your achievements, incorporate them into your actions subtly. Let your work speak for itself.

Overly drawing attention to your success can make it seem forced or less impressive.

- **Be Nonchalant About Success**: When you succeed, remain humble and nonchalant. Act as if your achievements were just another part of your routine. This conveys confidence and power while making your efforts appear effortless.
- **Minimize Complaints or Self-Congratulation**: Avoid complaining about challenges or excessively praising your own accomplishments. Instead, let your results stand on their own merit, without the need for validation or acknowledgment. This enhances the perception that you succeed with ease.
- **Refine Your Skills to Perfection**: The more you refine your abilities, the more naturally they will come to you. Mastery of your craft reduces the effort required to perform and helps you maintain the illusion that your success is effortless.
- **Cultivate an Air of Mystery**: Keep some aspects of your process or journey secret. By withholding information about the work behind your success, you create intrigue and enhance the perception that your achievements are the result of innate talent or luck, rather than effort.

Recognizing When Others Use It

- They rarely discuss challenges or difficulties.
- They avoid showing stress or fatigue.
- They downplay the time spent on a task.
- They keep their planning process private.
- They display calm confidence in high-stakes situations.
- They avoid asking for help or appearing overwhelmed.
- They act as though success was inevitable.
- They deliver results with an air of ease.
- They subtly discourage praise for hard work.
- They focus on the outcome rather than the process.

How to Neutralize Its Use

- Recognize that effort may be hidden; don't underestimate them.
- Acknowledge your own accomplishments without comparison.
- Focus on your own standards rather than others' perceptions.

- Observe their methods to understand their process.
- Keep in mind that their "ease" may not reflect reality.
- Balance confidence with self-awareness.
- Respect their achievements while focusing on your goals.
- Share your process with those who support you.
- Value hard work and patience over instant results.
- Avoid feeling pressured to match an idealized standard.

Behaviors that Make You a Target

- **Constantly Bragging About Your Effort**: If you frequently talk about how hard you worked or how much effort you put into a task, you reveal the labor behind your success. This diminishes the perception of your accomplishments being effortless and makes you appear vulnerable to manipulation by those who may downplay your hard work.
- **Over-Explaining Your Process**: If you go into excessive detail about how you achieved your success, it removes the mystery and allure. This makes your achievements seem more like the result of calculation and hard work rather than innate skill or effortless talent, making you more predictable and easier to manipulate.
- **Being Too Transparent About Challenges**: Constantly discussing the difficulties you've faced makes you appear less capable and less impressive. If people see how hard it was for you to succeed, they may doubt your ability and start questioning your power or competence, making you an easier target for manipulation.
- **Showing Visible Signs of Stress or Strain**: If others can see that you are struggling or stressed, they may perceive you as weaker or less in control. This opens the door for others to take advantage of your vulnerability and manipulate you, as they will believe that your success wasn't as effortless as it seemed.
- **Excessively Seeking Validation or Praise**: If you are always seeking recognition or praise for your work, it undermines the image of effortless success. Others may see you as insecure or needy, which makes it easier for manipulative individuals to control your actions by offering or withholding validation.
- **Oversharing Your Failures or Mistakes**: Constantly talking about your failures or mistakes, particularly in public, can make you seem less capable.

People will then perceive your success as an accident rather than a result of skill, making it easier for others to manipulate you into taking the blame for future failures or setbacks.

- **Being Too Competitive**: If you constantly try to show off your superiority or compete with others, it can expose the effort you put into your achievements. This draws unnecessary attention to your struggles and makes you seem less naturally powerful, thus easier to manipulate by those who play on your insecurities.
- **Displaying Desperation for Success**: If you are constantly striving for approval or recognition, it shows that your achievements are a result of intense effort and desperation. This desperation makes you more vulnerable to manipulation, as others can exploit your need for validation and take advantage of your drive.
- **Letting Others See Your Insecurities**: If you reveal self-doubt or show uncertainty about your success, it weakens your position. Manipulators will exploit your insecurities to steer you off course, using your doubt to their advantage.
- **Failing to Control Your Narrative**: If you don't take control of how your successes are perceived, others can shape your story for you. If others are allowed to frame your success as a result of luck, privilege, or other factors, it undermines the perception of effortless achievement and opens you up to manipulation by those who want to redefine your value.

Part VII

Becoming Unstoppable

_____

Law 31: Control the Options: Get Others to Play the Cards You Deal

Frame choices so others naturally choose what serves you.

Law 32: Play to People's Fantasies

Offer inspiration to captivate others and gain their loyalty.

Law 33: Discover Each Man's Thumbscrew

Identify key motivations and use them wisely.

Law 34: Be Royal in Your Own Fashion: Act Like a King to Be Treated Like One

Carry yourself with confidence and authority.

Law 35: Master the Art of Timing

Strike at the right moment to maximize your impact.

Law—**31**

Control the Options: Get Others to Play with the Cards You Deal

"If you want to control someone, all you have to do is to make them feel afraid."

— *Paulo Coelho*

Law 31: Control the Options: Get Others to Play with the Cards You Deal

This law advises controlling situations by offering limited choices, directing people toward decisions that ultimately serve your interests. By framing the options, you maintain control over their actions.

The Power Behind the Principle

When people feel they have choices, they are more likely to comply, even if those choices are influenced. Offering options also reduces resistance, making others feel they are in control. The benefit is subtly guiding others without overt pressure.

Putting It to Use

- **Present Limited Choices**: When you need others to make a decision, provide them with only a few options—preferably options that lead to the outcome you desire. By narrowing their choices, you maintain control over the situation, ensuring they pick the path most advantageous to you.
- **Make Your Offer Appealing**: Ensure that the options you offer are framed in a way that makes them seem attractive and desirable. By presenting one option as the clear and most advantageous choice, you increase the chances that others will pick it, unaware that they are essentially being steered toward your preferred outcome.
- **Create False Dilemmas**: Present two options that are both beneficial to you but make them seem like the only possible choices. This forces others to choose between the lesser of two evils or seemingly reasonable alternatives, both of which ultimately serve your interests.
- **Give the Illusion of Freedom**: Allow people to believe they are making their own choices by making the options seem open-ended. Let them feel that they are in control, even though you've set the framework of the decision-making process. This gives them a sense of agency while keeping them within your bounds.
- **Use Anchoring**: Start by offering an extreme option to set the stage, and then present your preferred choice as a much more reasonable alternative.

The person will then feel that they are making a balanced decision when, in reality, they have been subtly influenced by your initial „anchor" point.

- **Create a Sense of Urgency**: Introduce urgency to limit the available time for decision-making. When people feel rushed, they are less likely to thoroughly evaluate their options and more likely to choose based on the pressure you've applied, which can push them into selecting a choice that benefits you.
- **Frame Choices as Wins**: Even when the options seem to be about offering a „compromise," ensure that all choices appear to be advantageous. This makes others feel as though they are winning, which increases their willingness to accept your terms, even if the options are all skewed in your favor.
- **Restrict Information**: Control the flow of information. Only give others the information they need to make decisions that benefit you. By limiting what they know, you influence their choices, ensuring that they can't fully see the larger picture or make an informed decision that might go against your interests.
- **Create a False Sense of Competition**: Present multiple options or paths that seem to be in competition with each other, but in reality, they all lead to the same goal: your preferred outcome. This can make others feel like they are in control of their destiny, while in truth, they are merely playing along with your prearranged game.
- **Set the Terms of Negotiation**: When entering negotiations or discussions, establish the parameters or rules for engagement before the other party can offer their input. By controlling the framework within which the conversation occurs, you set the terms that benefit you, making it more likely that others will accept your proposals.

Recognizing When Others Use It

- They frequently offer limited options.
- They avoid presenting "no" as an option.
- They frame situations in ways that favor their goals.
- They act open to input but steer the choices subtly.
- They make suggestions that direct you to desired outcomes.
- They present only the most favorable paths.
- They emphasize the "benefits" of each choice.
- They avoid situations where you could decline entirely.
- They influence perceptions of each option.

- They remain calm, allowing you to "choose."

How to Neutralize Its Use

- Assess all possible alternatives independently.
- Take time to analyze options before deciding.
- Recognize any patterns in their approach.
- Consider if there are unstated options available.
- Ask questions to clarify your true choices.
- Balance their suggestions with objective perspectives.
- Maintain control over your decision-making process.
- Avoid feeling pressured to choose immediately.
- Seek advice from neutral parties if uncertain.
- Trust your instincts if their influence feels limiting.

Behaviors that Make You a Target

- **Being Too Open to All Options**: If you leave everything open and don't set boundaries, others can take advantage of your indecision. By offering too many choices without controlling the outcome, you give away your power, making it easier for others to steer you in the direction that benefits them.
- **Showing Indecisiveness**: If you are indecisive or constantly unsure about which option to take, you invite others to take control of the decision-making process. This makes it easy for them to manipulate you by subtly guiding you toward their preferred option, while making you believe it's your choice.
- **Giving Away Too Much Information**: If you provide all the information upfront or allow others to ask unlimited questions, you relinquish control over the negotiation or decision-making process. Manipulators thrive on knowing more than you do, and by giving away too much, you make it easy for them to create a situation where the options seem to favor them.
- **Not Setting Clear Boundaries**: If you don't establish clear boundaries or limits, others will feel free to push you in any direction. This can leave you open to manipulation, as people will try to make decisions for you within the space you've left unprotected, leading to outcomes that don't serve your best interests.
- **Seeking Validation or Consensus**: If you seek constant validation or require consensus from others before making decisions, you leave yourself open to

manipulation. Those who know this about you will push you toward options that align with their goals, often framing it as a „group decision" when, in fact, they have already made up their minds for you.

- **Relying on Others for Decision-Making**: If you constantly rely on others to help you make decisions, you give up your autonomy. Manipulators can influence you by presenting options that seem appealing, all while ensuring that you don't realize they've carefully orchestrated the entire process.
- **Not Planning Ahead**: If you fail to anticipate the possible outcomes of different options, you are more vulnerable to being pushed into a corner. Lack of foresight leaves you susceptible to manipulation, as you won't see the consequences of the options being presented to you until it's too late.
- **Showing Desperation or Weakness**: If you show desperation, insecurity, or uncertainty in decision-making, others will take advantage of your vulnerability. This behavior invites manipulation, as people will offer solutions that benefit them, while masking their own self-interest as helping you.
- **Giving Others Control Over Resources**: If you allow others to control your resources (time, money, information, etc.), they can limit your options and manipulate you into making choices that are advantageous to them. This can include everything from financial dependence to relying on others for critical advice or information.
- **Being Too Passive in Negotiations**: If you don't actively participate in shaping the terms of a negotiation or decision-making process, you make it easy for others to dictate the direction. A passive approach invites manipulation, as others will take control and guide you toward their preferred outcome.

Law—**32**

Play to People's Fantasies

"Reality is wrong. Dreams are for real."

— *Tupac Shakur*

Law 32: Play to People's Fantasies

This law advises tapping into people's dreams or ideals rather than their reality. By appealing to their aspirations, you can capture their interest and loyalty, often more effectively than through practicality.

The Power Behind the Principle

People are often driven by desires and dreams, and appealing to these fantasies creates an emotional connection. They are more likely to support you if they believe you can help them achieve these ideals. The benefit is influence over others through an appeal to their aspirations.

Putting It to Use

- **Offer Idealistic Solutions**: Present solutions to problems in a way that aligns with people's dreams or fantasies. Instead of offering practical, hard work-based solutions, emphasize ideal outcomes that make people feel like they can easily achieve their desires, no matter how unrealistic.
- **Use Inspirational Language**: Frame your words and ideas in a way that inspires and uplifts. Use language that appeals to people's dreams, hopes, and aspirations. This can make them feel that they are on the verge of achieving something great, without having to face the harsh realities.
- **Create a Vision of a Better Future**: Offer a vision of the future that appeals to the collective fantasy of your audience. Whether it's the promise of wealth, success, or personal transformation, paint a picture of a future that is better than the present, and make people believe that it's possible to achieve.
- **Use Mystique and Enigma**: Don't give away too much about yourself or your true intentions. Instead, keep an air of mystery around your persona, which can make you appear more alluring. People will be drawn to the fantasy of who you could be and will project their desires onto you.
- **Make Them Feel Special**: People want to feel unique and important. By making them believe that they have access to exclusive knowledge, opportunities, or experiences, you tap into their desire for special treatment and make them more likely to follow your lead.

- **Sell Hope**: Promise hope and transformation, especially during times of crisis or uncertainty. Whether through your ideas, products, or services, make it seem like you can provide a way out of despair or help others realize their deepest desires.
- **Appeal to Ego and Vanity**: Play to people's fantasies about their own greatness. Flatter them, tell them they have untapped potential, or remind them of their hidden brilliance. By appealing to their fantasies about their abilities or future, you create a stronger bond and gain influence.
- **Create Escapism**: Offer a way for people to escape the dullness of their everyday lives. Whether through entertainment, adventure, or fantasies of success, make them believe that your offerings can take them somewhere better or more exciting than where they are now.
- **Promise a "Shortcut" to Success**: People often want to avoid the hard work and struggle that accompanies success. By offering a seemingly easy path to wealth, power, or happiness, you align with their fantasies of achieving their goals without facing the usual obstacles.
- **Reinforce Their Beliefs**: Play to people's pre-existing fantasies and beliefs about the world, themselves, or their future. By reinforcing these fantasies, you give them a sense of validation and make it more likely that they will support you or adopt your ideas, as it aligns with what they already wish were true.

Recognizing When Others Use It

- They emphasize visions of the future over practical steps.
- They talk about ideals and "what could be."
- They downplay obstacles or challenges.
- They offer a romanticized view of situations.
- They emphasize your potential rather than the present.
- They focus on aspirations rather than realism.
- They share stories that evoke hope or excitement.
- They avoid discussing concrete details.
- They encourage you to think beyond present limitations.
- They avoid talking about risks.

How to Neutralize Its Use

- Evaluate ideas with a grounded perspective.
- Recognize when excitement overrides rational thought.
- Stay objective and focus on real-world outcomes.
- Assess their ideas based on feasibility.
- Avoid letting emotions influence critical decisions.
- Ask for concrete details and evidence.
- Balance optimism with practicality.
- Recognize when aspirations may be unrealistic.
- Set realistic expectations for results.
- Keep long-term consequences in mind.

Behaviors that Make You a Target

- **Being Disillusioned with Reality**: If you are dissatisfied with your current situation or the world around you, you may be more susceptible to someone who offers you a fantasy. Manipulators often prey on people who are dissatisfied with their reality by presenting an idealized version of what could be.
- **Constantly Seeking Validation**: If you are constantly looking for validation from others about your potential or success, you are likely to fall prey to those who flatter you or make grand promises that align with your fantasies. You become more likely to follow someone who feeds into your dreams of grandeur.
- **Overindulging in Escapism**: If you often escape into daydreams, entertainment, or fantasy, you are more likely to be manipulated by someone who can offer you a more vivid or exciting fantasy. Escapism can create an opening for those who promise to make your dreams come true without asking for hard work in return.
- **Being Overly Idealistic**: If you constantly seek perfect solutions and refuse to accept the imperfections of life, you open yourself up to being manipulated by those who promise perfect solutions or offer unrealistic expectations about how to achieve your goals.
- **Believing in Quick Fixes**: If you tend to believe in easy shortcuts or quick fixes, you make yourself vulnerable to manipulation by those who promise fast success, instant wealth, or effortless transformation. By failing

to acknowledge the hard work required, you can be led astray by empty promises.

- **Desiring Instant Gratification**: If you constantly seek immediate rewards and lack patience, you may fall for people who promise you quick, dramatic results. This desire for instant gratification makes it easier for manipulators to lure you with illusions of fast success, wealth, or recognition.
- **Lacking Self-Awareness**: If you don't have a clear sense of your own limitations or desires, you are more likely to be influenced by others who appeal to your fantasies. Without a grounded sense of reality, you can easily be swayed by those who promise to help you achieve unattainable dreams.
- **Not Questioning Authority or Promises**: If you blindly follow authority figures or accept promises without questioning their feasibility, you allow others to manipulate your fantasies. By failing to critically evaluate the promises being made to you, you are more likely to fall for manipulative tactics that appeal to your hopes and dreams.
- **Chasing Perfection**: If you are obsessed with achieving perfection or an idealized version of success, you can be easily led astray by those who promise that their way is the shortcut to that perfection. People who promise you an ideal future that aligns with your fantasies will exploit your perfectionist tendencies.
- **Being Vulnerable Due to Fear or Anxiety**: If you are feeling fearful, anxious, or uncertain about your future, you are particularly vulnerable to those who offer an escape through fantasy. Manipulators can take advantage of your emotional state, offering you visions of hope or success that may be unrealistic, making you more likely to follow them.

*Law—***33**

Discover Each Man's Thumbscrew

"Give me a lever long enough and a fulcrum on which to place it, and I shall move the world."

— Archimedes

Law 33: Discover Each Man's Thumbscrew

This law advises identifying people's weaknesses or desires that make them vulnerable. By understanding what drives others, you can leverage this insight to influence or control them.

The Power Behind the Principle

Everyone has a "thumbscrew"—a point of sensitivity or motivation. Recognizing these drivers enables you to connect with or manipulate others more effectively. The benefit is increased influence over others by appealing to their vulnerabilities.

Putting It to Use

- **Observe Body Language and Behavior**: Pay close attention to how people act and react. Often, a person's true feelings and vulnerabilities are expressed non-verbally. Look for signs of discomfort, nervousness, or defensiveness, which may reveal their fears or insecurities. These are often clues to their "thumbscrew."
- **Ask Subtle Questions**: During conversations, ask questions that allow people to talk about themselves in a way that reveals their desires or fears. People are often more open than they realize and will provide information that you can later use to gain an advantage or apply pressure.
- **Engage in Empathy to Build Trust**: Develop rapport by showing genuine empathy. When people feel comfortable with you and believe you understand them, they may inadvertently reveal their vulnerabilities or concerns, which you can use to gain influence over them.
- **Identify Emotional Weaknesses**: Understand the emotional triggers that affect people—whether it's their ego, self-esteem, or fear of failure. Once you identify what makes someone emotional or vulnerable, you can use these emotional „thumbscrews" to influence their decisions and actions.
- **Watch for Patterns in Their Actions**: Look for recurring behaviors that stem from deep-rooted desires or fears. For example, someone who consistently seeks approval may be manipulated by promises of recognition or validation, while someone who fears losing status may be controlled by threats to their position.

- **Use Flattery to Expose Vulnerabilities**: Give compliments that are just enough to make someone feel important or validated, and observe how they respond. Flattery can reveal people's need for approval or attention, which can be exploited to subtly control or manipulate them.
- **Study Their Past**: People's past experiences, especially childhood or formative years, often shape their vulnerabilities. By learning about someone's background, you may discover unresolved issues or unmet desires that can be used to influence their actions or decisions.
- **Create Situations that Test Their Weaknesses**: Put individuals in positions where their vulnerabilities or desires are likely to surface. For instance, offering them a tempting opportunity or subtle pressure can force them to reveal their weaknesses, allowing you to understand how to manipulate them.
- **Appeal to Their Desires**: Everyone has desires, whether it's for wealth, power, security, or recognition. Once you understand what drives someone, you can offer them something that aligns with those desires, positioning yourself as a source of fulfillment and control.
- **Monitor Their Reactions to Stress**: Observe how people behave under pressure or in stressful situations. Their reactions will often give away what they fear or desire most. For example, someone who panics under stress may have an underlying fear of failure, and you can leverage that fear to gain influence over them.

Recognizing When Others Use It

- They ask probing, personal questions.
- They show interest in your passions or frustrations.
- They observe your reactions to different topics.
- They remember personal details you've shared.
- They bring up topics where you're emotionally invested.
- They create a sense of camaraderie based on shared values.
- They emphasize topics that evoke strong feelings.
- They use supportive language to gain your trust.
- They subtly bring up weaknesses in conversation.
- They offer help in areas where you feel uncertain.

How to Neutralize Its Use

- Recognize your own sensitivities and guard against them.
- Be mindful of revealing personal information.
- Observe their motives behind personal questions.
- Respond neutrally to sensitive topics.
- Limit what you share until trust is established.
- Build emotional resilience around your weak points.
- Question their reasons for focusing on certain topics.
- Maintain a balanced view of your strengths and weaknesses.
- Avoid confiding in those who may exploit it.
- Cultivate independence in areas where you feel vulnerable.

Behaviors that Make You a Target

- **Revealing Personal Insecurities**: If you openly share your fears, weaknesses, or insecurities with others, you make it easier for them to identify your vulnerabilities. Being too open about your emotional state or past failures can allow others to manipulate you by exploiting those weaknesses.
- **Chasing Validation**: Constantly seeking approval or recognition from others makes you susceptible to manipulation. If someone recognizes your need for validation, they can offer it when it suits them, or withhold it to control your actions or decisions.
- **Over-sharing Personal Information**: If you frequently talk about your personal life, desires, or fears, you expose yourself to manipulation. By giving people access to your private thoughts, they can identify emotional triggers or vulnerabilities they can later use against you.
- **Lacking Emotional Control**: If you are overly emotional or reactive, it signals that you are vulnerable to manipulation. People who can trigger your emotions—whether through compliments, criticism, or pressure—can gain leverage over you by exploiting your emotional responses.
- **Being Overly Ambitious**: If you express a strong desire for power, wealth, or recognition, people may identify your ambitions as a point of manipulation. Manipulators may promise opportunities, play on your desire for status, or use your ambitions as leverage to get you to act in their favor.
- **Demonstrating a Fear of Failure**: If you consistently show fear of failure, people can use that to control you. A fear of being seen as incompetent or

unsuccessful can lead you to make decisions based on anxiety, which can be exploited by those who understand this fear.

- **Seeking to Please Others**: If you have a strong desire to please or avoid conflict, people may see this as a vulnerability. Manipulators can take advantage of your need to avoid confrontation, subtly pressuring you to agree with them or make decisions that align with their goals.

- **Being Easily Flattered**: If you are prone to flattery or seek compliments, others may use this to control you. By recognizing your desire for praise, manipulators can feed your ego to make you more compliant with their desires or use your inflated sense of self to further their own agenda.

- **Having a Low Sense of Self-Worth**: If you lack self-confidence or self-esteem, you are more susceptible to manipulation. People who perceive this vulnerability can exploit your need for affirmation or approval, controlling you by making you feel inadequate or insecure.

- **Revealing Stress or Anxiety**: If you openly show signs of stress or anxiety in certain situations, others will understand that you may be vulnerable to pressure. People who know what makes you anxious can use that knowledge to apply stress when they need to influence your actions or decisions.

Law—**34**

Be Royal in Your Own Fashion: Act Like a King to Be Treated Like One

"The world steps aside for the man who knows where he is going."

— *James Allen*

Law 34: Be Royal in Your Own Fashion: Act Like a King to Be Treated Like One

This law advises adopting the demeanor and confidence of someone who deserves respect. By acting with self-assurance and dignity, others are more likely to treat you with deference and respect.

The Power Behind the Principle

People tend to follow those who project authority and self-worth. By behaving as if you expect respect, others may be influenced to treat you accordingly. The benefit is that you establish yourself as a respected presence, gaining influence and esteem.

Putting It to Use

- **Exude Confidence in Your Actions**: Project a sense of confidence in everything you do. Whether you're walking into a room or engaging in a conversation, carry yourself with purpose and self-assuredness. Confidence signals power and attracts respect from others.
- **Maintain High Standards for Yourself**: Act with dignity by maintaining a high standard of conduct. Do not settle for mediocrity or allow others to treat you poorly. By setting standards for how you expect to be treated, others will be compelled to treat you accordingly.
- **Control Your Emotions**: A royal figure never shows weakness through uncontrolled emotions. Practice emotional discipline, and do not let anger, anxiety, or insecurity dictate your behavior. Maintaining composure in challenging situations projects strength and power.
- **Dress the Part**: Your appearance plays a significant role in how others perceive you. Dressing well and with purpose sends the message that you have high standards and expect to be treated with respect. Clothing is an outward sign of inner confidence and self-worth.
- **Stand Firm in Your Decisions**: Be decisive and stand firm in your beliefs and choices. Royalty does not second-guess itself or waver under pressure. By making decisions confidently and sticking to them, you demonstrate control and authority.

- **Cultivate an Air of Mystery**: Like royalty, maintain an aura of mystery about yourself. Don't reveal all your thoughts, feelings, or intentions. By keeping some things to yourself, you create intrigue, which increases your perceived value and power.
- **Engage in Self-Improvement**: Constantly work on your personal development, whether it's through education, skill acquisition, or fitness. A king or queen is always evolving and improving. By striving to be the best version of yourself, you increase your own sense of self-worth and project power to others.
- **Be Generous with Your Presence**: People respect those who value their own time and presence. Make your time and attention feel like a gift to others. When you are selective about when and where you offer your attention, people will value and respect your presence more.
- **Speak with Authority**: When you speak, do so with clarity, confidence, and authority. Use your voice to convey strength, and avoid being overly deferential or apologetic. A commanding presence in conversation enhances your status and encourages others to listen and respect you.
- **Be Independent**: Develop a sense of independence and self-sufficiency. A royal figure does not depend on others for validation or support; they stand on their own. By cultivating your own resources, knowledge, and skills, you present yourself as someone who doesn't need others' approval to thrive.

Recognizing When Others Use It

- They exhibit a high level of confidence.
- They maintain a composed and dignified demeanor.
- They avoid compromising situations or actions.
- They display a sense of entitlement to respect.
- They remain calm under pressure, projecting strength.
- They assert themselves without aggression.
- They dress or present themselves well.
- They avoid acting subserviently.
- They demand fair treatment without pleading.
- They maintain high standards for themselves and others.

How to Neutralize Its Use

- Avoid feeling intimidated by their demeanor.
- Set boundaries if their behavior becomes demanding.
- Recognize confidence but evaluate their actions objectively.
- Treat them with respect but maintain self-assurance.
- Avoid excessive admiration; focus on mutual goals.
- Keep interactions professional and balanced.
- Appreciate confidence without feeling overshadowed.
- Establish your own standards for interactions.
- Avoid falling into a deferential role.
- Focus on the value of the work rather than their persona.

Behaviors that Make You a Target

- **Displaying Insecurity**: If you show signs of insecurity, doubt, or indecisiveness, people may treat you as lesser. Insecurity can make you appear weak or easily influenced, making it more likely that others will try to manipulate you for their benefit.
- **Seeking Constant Validation**: If you are constantly seeking approval or validation from others, you open yourself up to manipulation. When you rely on others for your sense of worth or self-esteem, you create a situation where others can control or manipulate you by withholding their validation.
- **Apologizing Excessively**: Over-apologizing for small mistakes or things that aren't your fault sends the message that you lack confidence and self-respect. This can make others feel that they can walk all over you, as they perceive you as someone who will constantly yield to their demands.
- **Allowing Others to Dictate Your Decisions**: If you frequently let others decide for you or allow them to push you into decisions you don't truly want, you give up your own power and autonomy. Manipulative individuals will exploit this tendency, taking advantage of your lack of assertiveness.
- **Lack of Personal Boundaries**: If you allow others to constantly infringe on your time, energy, or space without setting clear boundaries, you make yourself vulnerable to being taken advantage of. People are less likely to treat you with respect if you don't demand it through your actions and words.

- **Showing Desperation for Attention**: If you constantly seek attention or act desperate for recognition, people will perceive you as needy and weak. Desperation signals that you don't value yourself enough to command respect, making it easier for others to manipulate you.
- **Being Too Flexible or Yielding**: If you lack the ability to stand firm in your decisions or constantly yield to the desires of others, you give up your power. People who sense that you will go along with whatever they want can use this to manipulate you into serving their interests.
- **Being Easily Impressed or Flattered**: If you are easily flattered or swayed by compliments and praise, you open yourself to manipulation. Those who flatter you with the intent to control will gain influence over you by exploiting your need for affirmation.
- **Showing Weakness Through Emotional Outbursts**: If you frequently display emotional weakness—such as crying, anger, or anxiety—others may lose respect for you. Manipulators can prey on your emotional outbursts, using them to influence your decisions or make you feel vulnerable and dependent on them.
- **Compromising Your Integrity**: If you consistently compromise your values or ethics in order to gain approval or avoid conflict, you lose your inner authority. When you sacrifice your integrity, you show others that you do not value yourself, making you more susceptible to manipulation.

*Law—***35**

Master the Art of Timing

"Time is a created thing. To say 'I don't have time' is to say 'I don't want to.' "

— Lao Tzu

Law 35: Master the Art of Timing

This law suggests carefully timing your actions, waiting for the most opportune moments to move forward. Knowing when to act and when to pause is key to achieving success without resistance.

The Power Behind the Principle

Timing can determine the success of an action, as acting too early or too late can diminish its impact. Patience and attentiveness allow you to choose moments of maximum advantage. The benefit is that you can seize opportunities effectively, while minimizing obstacles.

Putting It to Use

- **Observe and Assess the Situation**: Take time to assess the landscape before making any decisions. Don't rush into action—carefully evaluate the situation and wait for the right opportunity to present itself. By observing others and the environment, you can make a more informed decision.
- **Know When to Be Patient**: Sometimes the most powerful move is to do nothing at all. By exercising patience, you allow the situation to evolve naturally, often in your favor. People may reveal their true intentions or weaknesses over time, making it easier for you to act when the moment is right.
- **Learn to Read the Room**: Pay close attention to the emotions, dynamics, and energy in the room. People's body language, tone of voice, and responses to others will give you clues about when to make your move. Understanding the subtle emotional undercurrents can help you know when to act or when to wait.
- **Delay Action to Increase Your Leverage**: Sometimes holding off on a decision or action can increase your power and influence. The longer you wait, the more tension builds, and the more eager others become for resolution. This gives you a greater ability to control the terms of the situation when you finally make your move.
- **Don't Reveal Your Hand Too Soon**: Keep your plans and intentions hidden until the right moment. By revealing too much too early, you lose the element

of surprise. Timing your revelations—whether of your power, skills, or intentions—gives you greater control and impact.

- **Know When to Retreat**: Mastering timing involves knowing when to step back and wait for a more favorable moment. If the time isn't right, retreating can allow you to live to fight another day, preserving your resources and energy for a more opportune moment.
- **Seize the Moment**: When the right opportunity arises, take immediate and decisive action. Mastering timing means not hesitating when the time is ripe. If you wait too long, someone else may take advantage of the opportunity, so you must act swiftly when the time is right.
- **Cultivate Patience for Long-Term Gains**: Often, timing is about playing the long game. Master the ability to wait for the right moment to leverage your power for maximum impact, even if it requires delayed gratification. Patience pays off, especially in situations that require a sustained effort to influence outcomes.
- **Take Advantage of People's Weak Moments**: People can be vulnerable at certain moments—whether when they're tired, stressed, or emotionally compromised. Recognizing these moments and knowing when to act can give you an edge. Wait for these windows of vulnerability and make your move when others are most susceptible.
- **Use the Power of Silence**: Sometimes, saying nothing at all is the most powerful move. Silence can build anticipation, pressure others to act, and force them to reveal information they wouldn't have otherwise. Knowing when to remain silent can often be as potent as knowing when to speak.

Recognizing When Others Use It

- They rarely rush into decisions or actions.
- They seem attuned to the atmosphere and context.
- They wait for optimal conditions before making moves.
- They are patient in negotiations or discussions.
- They show awareness of social or political dynamics.
- They avoid overreacting or impulsive actions.
- They observe and assess before acting.
- They seize moments of vulnerability in opponents.
- They appear composed and unhurried.
- They allow others to reveal their intentions first.

How to Neutralize Its Use

- Recognize the power of timing in your own actions.
- Avoid being pressured into premature decisions.
- Monitor their actions to anticipate future moves.
- Keep your own timing unpredictable.
- Don't reveal all your plans too early.
- Stay adaptable and responsive to changing conditions.
- Set clear deadlines to prevent manipulation by delay.
- Balance patience with assertiveness.
- Recognize when hesitation may be tactical.
- Avoid overestimating their control over timing.

Behaviors that Make You a Target

- **Acting Impulsively**: Rushing into action without considering the timing of your move can make you vulnerable to manipulation. People can exploit your haste and use your lack of patience against you by manipulating the situation or taking advantage of your premature actions.
- **Showing Desperation to Act**: If you show that you are eager or desperate to act, others may sense this vulnerability and use it to manipulate you into making hasty decisions. Manipulators may intentionally delay their responses or take advantage of your impatience to get you to make a poor decision.
- **Revealing Your Plans Too Early**: If you share your plans or intentions too soon, you lose the element of surprise, and others can adjust their actions accordingly. This allows them to manipulate the timing to their benefit, undermining your strategy and causing you to lose control of the situation.
- **Ignoring Signals and Waiting Too Long**: If you wait too long to act, you risk losing momentum or allowing others to take advantage of the opportunity. Overthinking or delaying your decision can cause you to miss the optimal time to act, leaving you in a weaker position.
- **Over-committing to One Course of Action**: Once you commit fully to a course of action, you may become rigid and less adaptable. If circumstances change and the timing is no longer right, your inability to adjust your course can make you vulnerable to those who are more flexible or able to take advantage of the new timing.

- **Failing to Read the Room**: If you don't assess the emotional dynamics of a situation or fail to recognize the right moment to act, you risk making moves at the wrong time. Others will exploit your inability to gauge the timing, manipulating the situation in ways that leave you out of control.
- **Being Overconfident or Over-enthusiastic**: If you act too confidently or with too much enthusiasm, you might come off as predictable and transparent. Others can manipulate your confidence to set you up for failure or take advantage of your eagerness to act.
- **Being Impatient or Frustrated**: Showing signs of impatience or frustration makes it clear that you're ready to act at any moment. This gives others the opportunity to push you into making a premature move that could undermine your position or power, allowing them to control the pace of events.
- **Revealing Your Vulnerability in Stressful Times**: When you're stressed or under pressure, you may be less capable of seeing the right moment to act. Your vulnerability can lead you to act too quickly, without considering the best timing. This creates openings for others to exploit your haste and make you act in their favor.
- **Letting Others Control the Pace**: If you allow others to set the pace of events or dictate when you should act, you lose control over the situation. People can manipulate the timing in their favor, making you react to their actions instead of taking the initiative and controlling the timing for yourself.

Part VIII

Sustaining Power Through Adaptability

Law 36: Disdain Things You Cannot Have: Ignoring Them is the Best Revenge
Don't let envy derail your focus.

Law 37: Create Compelling Spectacles
Use visuals and drama to inspire and captivate.

Law 38: Think as You Like but Behave Like Others
Stay authentic while navigating societal expectations.

Law 39: Stir up Waters to Catch Fish
Use disruption to create opportunities.

Law 40: Despise the Free Lunch
Invest in yourself and your worth.

Law— **36**

Disdain Things You Cannot Have: Ignoring Them is the Best Revenge

"If you can't have it, disdain it."

— *Publilius Syrus*

Law 36: Disdain Things You Cannot Have: Ignoring Them is the Best Revenge

This law advises that when you cannot achieve or control something, it's best to ignore it. By dismissing unattainable goals, you project power and control, reducing the importance of what you can't have.

The Power Behind the Principle

Obsession with the unattainable weakens your focus and makes you appear desperate. Ignoring what you cannot control shows strength and helps you focus on achievable goals. The benefit is freedom from frustration and a greater command over your resources.

Putting It to Use

- **Exude Indifference Toward What You Cannot Control**: Cultivate an air of indifference toward people or situations that are beyond your control. If something is unattainable or unavailable to you, act as if it holds no value. By ignoring it, you maintain the upper hand, as others will see that you are unaffected by it.
- **Avoid Showing Desire or Neediness**: Never let your desire for something unattainable show. Neediness or obvious longing for something you cannot have signals weakness. Instead, act as if it doesn't matter to you, even if internally you may feel disappointed.
- **Focus on What You Can Control**: Redirect your energy away from what you cannot have or change. Channel your attention into areas where you can have an impact and make progress. This reinforces your control and sends a signal that you are focused on your own destiny rather than things beyond your reach.
- **Play Down the Importance of What You Desire**: If there's something you want but cannot have, downplay its significance. Show that it is trivial or insignificant. By trivializing something you desire, you diminish its power over you and make it appear less important to others.
- **Use Silence and Inaction to Signal Disdain**: In many situations, silence can be a powerful tool. If something you cannot have is presented to you, refuse

to engage with it emotionally or verbally. Your silence signals to others that you aren't bothered by the absence or unavailability of that thing.

- **Express Contempt in a Subtle Manner**: If necessary, use subtlety to show that you disdain something you cannot have. A dismissive gesture, such as a roll of the eyes or a half-hearted comment, can communicate that you are not interested or impressed by what others consider valuable.
- **Don't Allow Yourself to Feel Envy**: Envy weakens you and makes you vulnerable to manipulation. Rather than feeling envious of something you cannot have, practice letting go of any envy you may feel. By accepting that some things are simply not meant for you, you maintain emotional strength.
- **Invest Your Energy in Other Desirable Goals**: Instead of fixating on something unattainable, focus on other goals or desires that are within your reach. By redirecting your ambitions, you not only avoid wasting energy on what you can't control but also give yourself a sense of accomplishment in areas where you can succeed.
- **Create a Sense of Superiority**: When others are obsessed with something unattainable, position yourself as someone who is above such desires. Act as though your contentment and self-sufficiency make you immune to the allure of the thing in question. This can intimidate others and reinforce your sense of superiority.
- **Control Your Response to Rejection**: If something or someone is unattainable (such as a promotion or a relationship), refuse to show any reaction to the rejection or denial. By accepting rejection without protest, you demonstrate emotional control and strength, making others respect your composure and poise.

Recognizing When Others Use It

- They avoid discussing goals that are out of reach.
- They appear indifferent to potential setbacks.
- They downplay challenges as unimportant.
- They focus on what they can control.
- They show resilience in the face of obstacles.
- They are selective about where they invest energy.
- They avoid reacting emotionally to losses.
- They seem unaffected by others' criticisms.
- They prioritize their own well-being over futile pursuits.

- They shift focus to areas with potential for success.

How to Neutralize Its Use

- Identify when their indifference may be strategic.
- Focus on your own goals without comparison.
- Avoid chasing unattainable goals out of envy.
- Set realistic targets for your progress.
- Recognize when to let go of diminishing returns.
- Respect their resilience without feeling diminished.
- Concentrate on your own achievements.
- Avoid reacting emotionally to their indifference.
- Seek areas where you can succeed without their influence.
- Value what is within your control.

Behaviors that Make You a Target

- **Showing Obvious Desire for What You Cannot Have**: If you overtly show longing for something unattainable, others may perceive this as a weakness. People can exploit your desire by dangling that unattainable thing in front of you, knowing you'll react emotionally or try to please them to get it.
- **Revealing Frustration Over Unattainable Goals**: Expressing frustration or disappointment about things you cannot have makes it clear that you are vulnerable. This emotional display signals to others that they can manipulate your feelings or motivations by offering false hope or teasing you with what you can't have.
- **Obsessing Over Things Beyond Your Reach**: Fixating on things that are unattainable only reinforces your lack of control. Obsession with things beyond your grasp can weaken your sense of power and make you susceptible to manipulation, as others may take advantage of your fixation.
- **Fighting for What You Can't Have**: If you keep pushing for something that you can't have, especially when it's clear it's out of your reach, you may appear desperate or weak. Manipulative individuals can use your persistence against you, offering false promises or drawing you into a futile pursuit.
- **Displaying Weakness or Vulnerability in the Face of Rejection**: If you react with visible disappointment or weakness when rejected or denied something you want, you signal that you are emotionally vulnerable. This invites others

to exploit your emotional state to manipulate you or use your desperation for their own purposes.

- **Compromising Your Principles to Gain Something Unattainable**: If you're willing to sacrifice your values or principles in order to obtain something you cannot have, it shows that you lack self-control and are easily manipulated. People can take advantage of your desperation by offering you false promises or by making you act in ways that undermine your integrity.
- **Chasing After Something Just to Prove a Point**: If your pursuit of something unattainable is driven by the need to prove something to others—whether it's your worth, intelligence, or status—you open yourself up to manipulation. Your need for validation can be exploited by those who know how to push your buttons.
- **Allowing Others to Dictate Your Desires**: If you let others tell you what you should want or desire, or let them shape your goals and aspirations, you may end up pursuing things that are unattainable for the sake of their influence. Manipulators can easily guide your decisions in their favor when you're not controlling your own desires.
- **Revealing Your Fear of Missing Out (FOMO)**: Expressing a fear of missing out on something you cannot have is a telltale sign of insecurity and weakness. This signals that you are vulnerable to manipulation by those who will exploit your FOMO to make you act rashly or take undesirable actions.
- **Engaging in Self-Pity or Martyrdom**: If you express pity for yourself because you can't have something you want, others may see you as weak and easy to manipulate. People who sense that you're feeling sorry for yourself might exploit that by offering false sympathy or promising something they have no intention of delivering.

Law— **37**

Create Compelling Spectacles

"Create your own style. Let it be unique for yourself and yet identifiable for others."

— Orson Welles

Law 37: Create Compelling Spectacles

This law advises that visual and theatrical displays can attract attention and build a memorable presence. By creating compelling spectacles, you captivate your audience and ensure your messages resonate.

The Power Behind the Principle

People are often drawn to vivid imagery and powerful visuals. Spectacles make you memorable, create a sense of awe, and increase your influence. The benefit is greater impact and attention, allowing your actions to stay in people's minds.

Putting It to Use

- **Leverage Dramatic Moments**: Use unexpected events, powerful gestures, or bold actions to make a lasting impression. When you're aiming to capture attention, make sure that your actions stand out—whether through a surprise move, an unexpected announcement, or a sudden shift in strategy.
- **Master the Art of Timing**: Timing is critical to making an impact. Wait for the right moment to create a spectacle—when people's attention is most needed or when the stakes are highest. A well-timed spectacle can elevate your position and increase the perception of your power.
- **Use Visual Impact**: Surround yourself with symbols of power or success that will make a visual impression on others. This could involve wearing distinctive clothing, using props or symbols that represent your authority, or staging dramatic entrances or exits. The visual presence reinforces your dominance.
- **Create Rituals or Traditions**: Establish rituals or traditions that become associated with you, your leadership, or your brand. People will look forward to these moments and associate them with your power and influence. Whether it's a unique way of making an announcement or a regular public display, these spectacles reinforce your stature.
- **Control the Narrative Through Symbolism**: Use powerful imagery and symbols to communicate messages without words. Whether through a powerful logo, striking colors, or specific gestures, symbolism can amplify your influence and make your presence memorable.

Combine Drama with Purpose: While dramatic moments are useful, they should always have a purpose. Don't make spectacles just for the sake of it—ensure that your actions or displays of grandeur communicate something meaningful about your goals, values, or vision. This way, people will respect the spectacle as part of a larger plan, not as empty theatrics.

- **Create an Aura of Mystery**: Part of creating a compelling spectacle is maintaining an air of mystery. Don't reveal all your plans at once. Leave people wanting more or guessing about your next move. This intrigue builds curiosity, which adds to your perceived power.
- **Use Your Environment to Amplify Your Image**: The environment you choose can contribute to creating a spectacle. Whether it's holding an important meeting in an iconic location, using lighting and sound to set the mood, or designing your office to exude power, the setting plays a key role in reinforcing your influence and the perception of your status.
- **Incorporate Drama into Communication**: When speaking, make your words count by delivering them dramatically. Use pauses, change of tone, and theatrical gestures to emphasize key points. A speech or conversation can become a spectacle in itself if it's delivered with intensity and precision.
- **Surprise and Shock Your Audience**: Create moments of surprise or shock to capture the attention of those around you. Whether it's a sudden change in direction, an unexpected alliance, or a bold declaration, these moments leave people reeling and make your actions stand out in their minds, enhancing your ability to lead and influence.

Recognizing When Others Use It

- They frequently use dramatic gestures or displays.
- They rely on visual elements to convey messages.
- They create memorable events or experiences.
- They focus on presentation as much as content.
- They draw large audiences or gatherings.
- They emphasize symbolism or metaphors.
- They act with theatrical flair to captivate attention.
- They avoid subtlety, favoring bold expressions.
- They use props, visuals, or staging to enhance their presence.
- They control the ambiance and setting of meetings or events.

How to Neutralize Its Use

- Focus on substance over presentation.
- Avoid being swayed by spectacle alone.
- Evaluate their message independently of theatrics.
- Maintain a level-headed perspective.
- Recognize when visuals are used to manipulate.
- Seek concrete details beyond the spectacle.
- Focus on practicality rather than theatrics.
- Set your priorities and avoid being distracted.
- Avoid investing in superficial impressions.
- Stay grounded and skeptical of exaggerated displays.

Behaviors that Make You a Target

- **Being Overly Predictable**: If you're predictable and always act the same way, people will stop paying attention. When you fail to create moments of surprise or excitement, you leave the door open for others to control the narrative or take the lead. People may begin to take you for granted and manipulate you because your reactions are too familiar.
- **Failing to Capture Attention**: If you blend into the background and don't make an effort to stand out, others may take advantage of your lack of presence. Without compelling spectacles or dramatic moments, you risk being overlooked, and others may manipulate situations where you lack the power or influence to change them.
- **Overuse of Simplicity**: While simplicity can be powerful, overusing it can make your presence forgettable. If you fail to inject any drama or intensity into your actions, people may overlook you and take advantage of your passive or straightforward nature. Your lack of spectacle can leave you vulnerable to manipulation by those who command more attention.
- **Being Easily Distracted by Small Matters**: When you focus too much on small details and neglect the larger picture, you miss opportunities to create significant moments that capture attention. Being too caught up in mundane tasks can distract you from the bigger picture and leave you exposed to others who know how to make their own spectacle and draw attention away from you.

- **Reacting to Criticism or Negativity**: If you constantly react defensively to criticism or negativity, you lose the ability to control your narrative. Others may manipulate your emotional reactions, forcing you into a position where you're constantly reacting instead of proactively creating compelling spectacles that build your image.
- **Lacking Boldness or Ambition**: If you're not bold or ambitious enough to stand out, others will take advantage of your passive nature. Failing to take calculated risks or make bold moves means you won't create the type of dramatic spectacles that command respect and attention, leaving you vulnerable to manipulation.
- **Allowing Yourself to Be Swayed by Public Opinion**: If you're constantly concerned with what others think, you lose the ability to create spectacles that work in your favor. People who are overly sensitive to public opinion or reactions are easily manipulated, as they become preoccupied with responding to external pressures rather than crafting their own narrative.
- **Failing to Capitalize on Opportunities for Dramatic Displays**: When opportunities arise to create a spectacle, failing to take advantage of them is a missed chance to control the narrative. If you shy away from opportunities to demonstrate power or leadership in dramatic ways, you allow others to make those moves and manipulate the situation in their favor.
- **Lack of Personal Branding or Image**: If you fail to develop a strong personal image or brand that makes you stand out, you leave yourself vulnerable. Without a distinctive identity or presence, you're easily overlooked, and others can manipulate situations where your lack of visibility or spectacle reduces your power and influence.
- **Being Stubborn or Unwilling to Adapt**: If you are too rigid and refuse to adapt your approach or persona, you lose the ability to create dynamic, compelling spectacles. Stubbornness can make you predictable and easy to manipulate by those who are flexible enough to create the spectacle that attracts attention and drives power.

*Law—*38

Think as You Like but Behave Like Others

"When in Rome, do as the Romans do."

— St. Ambrose

Law 38: Think as You Like but Behave Like Others

This law advises conforming outwardly to social norms and expectations, even if your private beliefs differ. By blending in, you avoid unnecessary conflict or scrutiny.

The Power Behind the Principle

People tend to resist those who openly challenge norms, so appearing aligned with the group allows you to avoid friction. You retain freedom of thought while ensuring smoother social interactions. The benefit is that you maintain independence without risking alienation.

Putting It to Use

- **Understand the Social Norms**: Carefully observe the behaviors and norms of those around you. Understand the expectations in social, business, or political environments, and adapt your behavior to fit in without drawing attention to yourself.
- **Blend In During Critical Moments**: When in groups or organizations, especially in high-stakes situations, tone down any behavior that might stand out. Whether it's dress code, body language, or communication style, make sure you don't appear different from others during moments of high visibility.
- **Master the Art of Mimicry**: Subtly mirror the body language, speech patterns, and mannerisms of those around you. This technique, known as „mirroring," can make you seem more agreeable and aligned with the people you interact with, thus gaining their trust and approval.
- **Conceal Your True Feelings**: Practice emotional restraint. Even if you disagree with something or feel strongly about an issue, mask your emotions to avoid confrontation. Keep your personal thoughts private, and don't express them openly if it might put you at odds with others.
- **Adapt Your Communication Style**: Speak in the same manner as those around you. If you're in a formal setting, be formal; in a more casual setting, use a more relaxed tone. Changing your communication style to match the group ensures you don't stand out and invites acceptance.
- **Avoid Extremes in Behavior**: Avoid being too radical in your opinions, especially in public settings. Extremes, whether in thoughts or actions, can

isolate you or make you appear untrustworthy. Stay balanced and avoid overly controversial positions unless absolutely necessary.

- **Learn to Flatter**: Flatter those in power or those whose opinions matter most to you. Express agreement with their points of view and defer to their opinions in public. This helps you fit in while also keeping the social peace.
- **Be the Chameleon**: Adapt to the culture of each environment. If you're in a business meeting, behave like a professional. In social situations, behave more casually and blend into the group. Adaptation is key to not drawing attention to yourself or your true feelings.
- **Follow the Leader**: When unsure about how to behave in a new environment, take your cues from the leader of the group. By observing and mirroring their actions, you can avoid making mistakes and ensure that you stay on the „right" side of things.
- **Stay Flexible in Your Opinions**: Be open to changing your views depending on the group you are in. While you don't have to sacrifice your core beliefs, it's wise to withhold or adjust your opinions to avoid unnecessary conflict or to gain acceptance in a new social environment.

Recognizing When Others Use It

- They act reserved about personal beliefs.
- They adapt to social settings and group norms.
- They avoid expressing dissenting opinions publicly.
- They show little reaction to divisive topics.
- They align outwardly with popular views.
- They avoid standing out in group settings.
- They adopt neutral expressions or gestures.
- They occasionally reveal different views in private.
- They maintain professional politeness in all interactions.
- They express thoughts only in trusted company.

How to Neutralize Its Use

- Recognize the value of conformity in social situations.
- Avoid pressing for personal views in public settings.
- Respect their desire for privacy on beliefs.
- Build rapport gradually to encourage openness.

- Encourage respectful dialogue, respecting boundaries.
- Avoid provoking unnecessary debates.
- Focus on commonalities rather than differences.
- Respect professional decorum and public standards.
- Recognize the role of social norms in interactions.
- Maintain your values without challenging their stance.

Behaviors that Make You a Target

- **Being Overly Confrontational or Opinionated**: If you frequently challenge the views or behaviors of others, especially those in power, you make yourself a target for manipulation. Those in control can use your confrontational nature against you, isolating you or making you seem disruptive.
- **Showing an Inability to Adapt to Social Contexts**: If you consistently behave in ways that are out of sync with the social environment you're in, you'll quickly stand out and be seen as an outsider. People will exploit your lack of adaptability, making it easier to manipulate or marginalize you.
- **Being Too Eager to Stand Out**: If you constantly try to distinguish yourself from the crowd—whether through eccentric behavior, bold opinions, or unique dress—you invite unwanted attention. Those who feel threatened by your differences can manipulate your desire for uniqueness to undermine your position.
- **Failing to Conceal Your True Intentions**: If you openly express your personal goals, desires, or strategies, others will use this knowledge to control or manipulate your actions. Keeping your inner thoughts hidden from others allows you to maintain the upper hand, while revealing too much makes you vulnerable.
- **Being Emotionally Unrestrained**: If you wear your emotions on your sleeve and frequently show frustration, anger, or disappointment, you risk making yourself an easy target. Manipulators will use your emotional volatility to provoke you into reactions that they can then exploit.
- **Overly Impressing with Your Individuality**: If you try too hard to show your individuality by going against the grain or distancing yourself from the group, you open yourself up to manipulation. Those who don't feel aligned with you may isolate you or use your desire to stand out to make you feel alienated.
- **Failing to Blend In When Necessary**: If you cannot read the room and refuse to adapt when necessary, you will find yourself out of place. Social dynamics

can shift rapidly, and if you don't blend in, you risk being sidelined or taken advantage of by those who are better able to adjust.

- **Not Conforming to Group Expectations**: When you fail to conform to group norms or expectations—whether it's in dress, language, or behavior—you can be marginalized. Manipulative people will take advantage of your refusal to conform and isolate you in the process.
- **Being Too Transparent in Your Behavior**: If you are too obvious in your desires or intentions, you give others the chance to take advantage of your transparency. Whether it's in business or social environments, those who are aware of your vulnerability or aspirations can manipulate you by using that knowledge against you.
- **Appearing Too Eager to Please**: If you always try to please others in an overt, obvious way, you give away your own power. Manipulators will sense your eagerness to conform and take advantage of your submissiveness by controlling or exploiting your actions for their own gain.

Law— **39**

Stir Up Waters to Catch Fish

"You must learn to provoke those you wish to control."

— Niccolò Machiavelli

Law 39: Stir Up Waters to Catch Fish

This law suggests creating confusion or turmoil to disrupt others' plans and take advantage of their disorientation. By stirring up waters, you gain an edge over those who become distracted or disoriented.

The Power Behind the Principle

Chaos makes it difficult for others to think clearly or focus, allowing you to manipulate situations to your advantage. The benefit is increased control and the ability to exploit others' loss of composure.

Putting It to Use

- **Create Distractions at Key Moments**: Introduce an element of chaos or confusion when important decisions are being made. This could involve raising an unrelated issue or making a bold statement that forces others to focus on you and your actions, giving you time to maneuver.
- **Introduce Uncertainty**: Instill doubt or uncertainty in others by questioning existing norms or decisions. By making people unsure about their environment or their next steps, you can cause them to hesitate or react impulsively, which can lead to mistakes that you can exploit.
- **Make Strategic Provocations**: Stir the pot by intentionally provoking someone or a group. A well-timed comment or action designed to upset a person or group can create emotional reactions, throwing them off balance and opening opportunities for you to act with less resistance.
- **Disrupt Calm Situations**: When things seem too peaceful or settled, introduce a new challenge, problem, or issue. A little disruption can break the complacency of others and give you a chance to capitalize on their uncertainty and confusion.
- **Set People Against Each Other**: Encourage competition or conflict between individuals or factions by spreading rumors or giving them contradictory information. If you can create division and discord between them, they will become distracted and weakened, leaving you free to maneuver.
- **Create False Conflicts or Divisions**: Raise minor issues into larger, seemingly important ones that cause people to lose focus on the bigger picture. By

creating these false conflicts, you force others to react, giving you a chance to control the flow of events from behind the scenes.

- **Stir Up Emotions**: Use emotional triggers—whether fear, greed, or jealousy—to cloud the judgment of others. By pushing their emotional buttons, you can make them act irrationally, allowing you to manipulate their decisions or actions.
- **Introduce Misdirection**: Divert attention away from your real objectives by introducing a different, more pressing issue. This will distract others and cause them to focus on the wrong problem, leaving you free to accomplish your goals without interference.
- **Create Chaos in Leadership**: If you're in a competitive situation, sow confusion among the leadership or decision-makers by introducing multiple contradictory ideas or positions. This can cause them to bicker and fail to make clear decisions, while you can work your way into a stronger position.
- **Use the Element of Surprise**: Introduce sudden, unexpected changes or challenges to disrupt the normal flow of events. By catching people off guard, you force them to react, allowing you to gain the upper hand or catch them off-balance.

Recognizing When Others Use It

- They introduce contentious topics to distract others.
- They act unpredictably, causing confusion.
- They bring up controversial issues at strategic moments.
- They often seem unbothered by chaos.
- They thrive in high-stress environments.
- They frequently change topics or plans abruptly.
- They avoid clarifying their motives or goals.
- They seek to create a sense of urgency.
- They use mixed messages or contradictory statements.
- They subtly encourage others to lose focus.

How to Neutralize Its Use

- Maintain calm and clarity, focusing on your objectives.
- Avoid engaging in distractions or controversies.
- Recognize when chaos is intentional.

- Refocus on priorities to avoid losing track.
- Observe their behavior without reacting emotionally.
- Minimize interactions in turbulent settings.
- Seek factual information over speculation.
- Prioritize rationality and steadiness.
- Avoid letting stress affect your decisions.
- Encourage stability and predictability in your team.

Behaviors that Make You a Target

- **Being Too Predictable or Routine**: If you always behave the same way or follow predictable patterns, others can easily predict your reactions and intentions. This makes you vulnerable to manipulation because others can stir up chaos to provoke a specific response from you, knowing exactly how you'll react.
- **Overlooking or Ignoring Small Disruptions**: If you ignore small disruptions or provocations, it allows the manipulator to escalate them. These minor disturbances, if left unchecked, can grow into larger issues that you may be forced to react to, often leading to confusion or mistakes.
- **Being Too Composed or Calm**: A person who is always calm and controlled might be seen as a target by those seeking to stir things up. If you never show emotion or a change in your demeanor, you may fail to recognize when others are subtly disrupting the situation to provoke a reaction.
- **Failing to Recognize Signs of Manipulation**: If you're not perceptive and fail to notice when others are trying to stir up trouble, you may find yourself caught in the chaos they create. Recognizing when someone is deliberately causing confusion allows you to act preemptively and regain control of the situation.
- **Overreacting to Provocations**: If you react emotionally or impulsively to small provocations, you become a target for manipulation. Those who can stir up your emotions will see that they can manipulate your behavior by triggering strong reactions that throw you off balance.
- **Being Too Focused on Status Quo**: If you're too committed to maintaining the current order or peaceful status quo, you may be vulnerable to disruption. Those who know how to stir the waters can use your resistance to change against you, throwing you into confusion when the unexpected happens.

- **Being Easily Distracted**: If you're easily distracted or quick to focus on minor issues, you invite manipulation. Those who wish to take advantage of you will introduce irrelevant problems or issues to divert your attention from the core situation, leaving you unable to focus on what's important.
- **Having Weak Leadership or Lack of Direction**: If you're in a leadership position but lack clarity or authority, you invite chaos. A lack of clear decision-making or inconsistent leadership creates opportunities for others to stir up problems and create confusion, which can then be exploited to challenge your position.
- **Avoiding Conflict**: If you're someone who avoids any form of conflict at all costs, others may manipulate your desire for peace. By stirring up conflict, they know you will back down or try to calm the situation, making it easier for them to push their agenda or take advantage of your discomfort.
- **Being Overly Honest or Transparent**: If you're too open and honest about your thoughts and plans, you allow others to stir up trouble by using that knowledge against you. Once they know your reactions, weaknesses, or plans, they can create confusion that forces you into a defensive position.

Law-**40**

Despise the Free Lunch

"There's no such thing as a free lunch."

— Milton Friedman

Law 40: Despise the Free Lunch

This law advises skepticism toward free offers, as they often come with hidden obligations or compromises. By valuing quality and refusing handouts, you maintain control and independence.

The Power Behind the Principle

Nothing is truly free, and accepting favors or gifts can create debts or obligations. Valuing what you pay for establishes self-reliance and prevents others from gaining leverage over you. The benefit is maintaining autonomy and control over your actions.

Putting It to Use

- **Set Clear, Uncompromising Goals**: Establish a crystal-clear vision of what victory looks like, and be unrelenting in your pursuit of it. If you're working on a project, political endeavor, or any competitive situation, ensure that your objectives are clear, measurable, and unyielding.
- **Pay Your Own Way**
  Cover the cost of your meals, tools, and training when possible. Independence earns respect and removes hidden obligations.
- **Invest in Your Skills**
  Buy your own books, courses, or certifications. When you invest personally, you value the knowledge more and no one can claim they "gave" it to you.
- **Decline Strings-Attached Favors**
  Be cautious when someone offers free help. If the "gift" creates a sense of debt or future expectation, politely decline.
- **Set Boundaries on Generosity**
  If someone insists on footing the bill, acknowledge the gesture but balance it later with a reciprocal act. Avoid feeling trapped in a lopsided exchange.
- **Choose Value Over Cost**
  Don't chase the cheapest option at work. Opt for what brings long-term benefit, even if it means an upfront investment.

- **Stay Wary of "Too Good to Be True"**
  Recognize that free perks, projects, or positions often come with invisible demands. Ask: What might this cost me later?
- **Fund Your Own Ambitions**
  Whether it's travel, networking, or side projects, save and invest in yourself. Ownership over your journey strengthens confidence and credibility.
- **Respect the Currency of Time**
  Remember that "free" often consumes time. Weigh whether accepting unpaid work, endless favors, or constant meetings is actually a hidden expense.
- **Show Gratitude Without Obligation**
  When you do accept a free resource, acknowledge it warmly but don't let gratitude become a leash. A thank-you is enough.
- **Model Empowered Exchange**
  Demonstrate that you believe in fair trade — your work, ideas, and effort have value, and so does the work of others. This normalizes mutual respect instead of hidden debt.

Recognizing When Others Use It

- They are selective about accepting offers or favors.
- They avoid situations where they might owe a favor.
- They prioritize quality and value over cost savings.
- They often pay their way to avoid dependency.
- They discourage others from offering handouts.
- They emphasize self-reliance in decision-making.
- They assess the motives behind "free" offers.
- They reject gifts that may come with strings attached.
- They appear wary of sudden generosity.
- They openly value what is earned over what is given.

How to Neutralize Its Use

- Avoid relying on their favors or free assistance.
- Recognize potential obligations hidden in offers.
- Be cautious of hidden costs or expectations.
- Maintain independence in accepting resources.
- Value quality and self-sufficiency over convenience.

- Decline offers that seem too good to be true.
- Politely avoid accepting unsolicited help.
- Pay for services to avoid being indebted.
- Focus on equal exchanges rather than free favors.
- Set boundaries to limit future expectations.

Behaviors that Make You a Target

- **Always Accepting Favors**
  If you constantly take "help" from colleagues or leaders, others may feel you owe them and expect repayment in loyalty or silence.
- **Letting Others Pay Your Way**
  Relying on others to cover costs for meals, events, or resources can create subtle obligations that weaken your independence.
- **Mistaking Free for Harmless**
  Assuming that "free" perks, training, or opportunities have no strings attached makes you vulnerable to hidden agendas.
- **Confusing Generosity with Support**
  Believing that a free favor equals genuine support can blind you to the leverage someone is creating over you.
- **Downplaying the Value of What Costs Money**
  Choosing the cheapest or free option every time signals that you don't value your own growth or future.
- **Relying on Sponsors Without Balance**
  If your career depends heavily on one person's backing, that sponsor may later dictate your moves or limit your independence.
- **Failing to Reciprocate**
  Accepting repeated generosity without balancing it creates a power imbalance where you're seen as indebted.
- **Overvaluing "Perks" Over Position**
  Focusing on free benefits or small favors instead of long-term advancement distracts from bigger goals and leaves you vulnerable.
- **Taking Shortcuts Instead of Investing**
  Choosing free or easy routes over paid, quality development shows a lack of seriousness, which others can exploit.

- **Ignoring the Hidden Costs of "Free"**
  Not asking, "What might this cost me later?" leaves you open to manipulation, as others cash in on debts you didn't realize you owed.

PART IX

The Power to Transform

Law 41: Avoid Stepping into a Great Man's Shoes
Avoid getting lost in someone else's legacy.

Law 42: Strike the Shepherd and the Sheep Will Scatter
Disarm key figures to strengthen your position.

Law 43: Work on the Hearts and Minds of Others
Build loyalty by connecting emotionally with others.

Law 44: Disarm and Infuriate with the Mirror Effect
Use their habits and strategies to your advantage.

Law 45: Preach the Need for Change, but Never Reform Too Much at Once
Balance bold ideas with measured actions.

Law—**41**

Avoid Stepping into a Great Man's Shoes

"Do not follow where the path may lead. Go instead where there is no path and leave a trail."

— Ralph Waldo Emerson

Law 41: Avoid Stepping into a Great Man's Shoes

This law advises against directly following in the footsteps of a highly successful predecessor. Instead, carve out your own identity to avoid being compared to them or overshadowed by their legacy.

The Power Behind the Principle

When you follow a legend, you risk failing to meet high expectations or appearing as a copy. Creating your own path sets you apart, allowing you to forge your own reputation. The benefit is avoiding constant comparison and building a distinct identity.

Putting It to Use

- **Create Your Own Identity**: Focus on developing your own unique strengths, skills, and characteristics that set you apart. Instead of mimicking a predecessor's style or tactics, make a mark that is distinctly yours. Find a niche where you can stand out without directly competing with someone else's legacy.
- **Embrace a Different Vision**: Instead of trying to continue a past leader's vision or follow their agenda, create your own vision for the future. This will allow you to chart your own course without being overshadowed by the past.
- **Avoid Direct Comparisons**: If you find yourself in a position where you must follow in the footsteps of a predecessor, avoid direct comparisons. Instead of being the „next" version of that person, present yourself as a unique individual with a different approach.
- **Build New Alliances**: Inheriting someone's role or legacy often means you will have to work with people who were loyal to that person. Rather than trying to simply pick up where they left off, create new alliances that are based on your strengths and ideas, rather than those of the predecessor.
- **Take a Fresh Approach**: If you are stepping into an influential position or role, avoid copying the strategies of the person who held it before you. Instead, bring in your own methods, strategies, and ways of thinking that reflect your personal style and values.

- **Focus on the Present and Future, Not the Past**: The past is a reference point, not an anchor. Focus on the present and future by adapting your actions to the current situation, instead of constantly looking backward and trying to preserve or recreate what was before.
- **Establish a New Standard**: Rather than trying to outdo a predecessor, set a new standard that is based on your own ideas and principles. By defining your own success criteria, you avoid the trap of comparison and allow yourself to build something unique.
- **Acknowledge the Legacy but Define Your Own Role**: If you must inherit a position, honor the legacy of the person who came before you but emphasize how you will be different. Acknowledge the past without being overwhelmed by it, and assert that you will bring your own perspective to the role.
- **Create Your Own Legacy**: Focus on establishing your own legacy rather than trying to surpass someone else's. Prioritize long-term goals and what you can build, rather than being preoccupied with living up to the standards set by another.
- **Be Comfortable in Your Own Skin**: Accept that no one can truly replace a great man. Embrace the fact that you are different, and that's okay. The more comfortable you are in your individuality, the less you will be bothered by comparisons, and the more you can carve out your own path.

Recognizing When Others Use It

- They avoid roles previously held by iconic figures.
- They create their own style or approach.
- They focus on establishing unique achievements.
- They avoid making direct comparisons to predecessors.
- They innovate rather than replicate.
- They emphasize their personal strengths.
- They sidestep conversations about prior leaders.
- They establish fresh ideas or initiatives.
- They create a distinct legacy rather than emulating others.
- They avoid direct competition with predecessors' achievements.

How to Neutralize Its Use

- Recognize their desire to create their own legacy.

- Avoid comparing them directly to previous figures.
- Encourage their unique contributions.
- Focus on their strengths rather than comparisons.
- Show openness to their new approach.
- Respect their need for originality.
- Avoid idolizing past achievements at their expense.
- Embrace the fresh perspective they bring.
- Support their unique goals and ideas.
- Set realistic expectations without referencing the past.

Behaviors that Make You a Target

- **Constantly Comparing Yourself to Others**: If you constantly compare yourself to a predecessor or another successful person, you will be constantly overshadowed. This makes you vulnerable to manipulation, as others will exploit your self-doubt and insecurities, using the predecessor's legacy to control you or undermine your decisions.
- **Imitating a Great Leader**: Trying to copy someone else's style or approach without understanding it fully can backfire. Imitation can make you appear inauthentic and predictable, which opens the door for others to exploit your lack of originality or individuality.
- **Clinging to the Past**: If you are constantly referencing the legacy of a predecessor, you fail to move forward and embrace the present moment. This makes you vulnerable to being manipulated by those who know how to use the past against you, creating distractions or false expectations based on an era that has already passed.
- **Being Overly Concerned with Reputation**: Trying too hard to live up to a predecessor's reputation or legacy can make you easily manipulated. Others may prey on your fear of failure or desire to be seen as „worthy," making you more susceptible to manipulation when you are constantly striving to meet an idealized image.
- **Attempting to Please Everyone**: If you try to win the approval of everyone who supported the predecessor or those with high expectations, you risk being pulled in too many directions. This leaves you open to being manipulated by different factions who may have their own agendas, using your desire to please as leverage.

- **Failing to Set Boundaries**: If you don't establish clear boundaries in your leadership or role, people will expect you to behave in ways that align with the predecessor's style. This opens the door for manipulation, as others may push you to act in ways that serve their interests rather than your own.
- **Being Overly Cautious or Hesitant**: If you're afraid to step out of the shadow of a predecessor, you may fail to make bold decisions. This hesitation can be exploited by others, who may manipulate you into taking the „safe" route, thus maintaining the status quo rather than taking a bold new direction.
- **Overcompensating for the Past**: If you try too hard to prove yourself by mimicking or surpassing what came before you, you may lose your sense of self. This opens the door for others to control you by playing on your insecurities, making you feel that you need to constantly „prove" your worth.
- **Refusing to Innovate**: If you simply try to repeat what was done before you, and fail to innovate or introduce new ideas, you may be manipulated by those around you. People will use your reluctance to change as a way to hold you back or keep you in a reactive role.
- **Lack of Self-Confidence**: If you do not believe in your ability to make your own mark and are always looking over your shoulder at the person who came before you, you invite manipulation. Others will use your lack of confidence to control your actions, create doubt in your decisions, and influence your thinking.

Law— **42**

Strike the Shepherd and the Sheep Will Scatter

"Remove the leader, and the rest will scatter."

— *Proverbs 11:14*

Law 42: Strike the Shepherd and the Sheep Will Scatter

This law advises neutralizing the primary source of opposition or dissent, as this weakens the resolve of those who follow them. Removing influential leaders diminishes the collective strength of their followers.

The Power Behind the Principle

By addressing the root of opposition, you minimize resistance and discourage followers from continuing the fight. This approach prevents further obstacles from forming. The benefit is reduced opposition and quicker control over a group.

Putting It to Use

- **Identify the Key Leader or Influencer**: Before attempting to disrupt a group, identify who holds the most power or influence within it. This could be an official leader, a charismatic figure, or someone who has a significant hold over others' decisions and actions.
- **Undermine the Leader's Authority**: Subtly or overtly undermine the leader's authority. This can be done by sowing doubt about their abilities, questioning their decisions, or highlighting their failures in front of the group. The goal is to weaken the leader's position without directly attacking them head-on.
- **Disrupt the Leader's Support Network**: If the leader is dependent on certain key allies, try to isolate them. Create divisions or conflicts within their support network, making it difficult for them to maintain a united front. Without loyal allies, the leader becomes much more vulnerable.
- **Target the Leader's Weaknesses**: Identify the leader's personal or professional weaknesses, whether emotional, financial, or reputational. Expose these vulnerabilities to the group to reduce the leader's credibility and to cause them to lose influence.
- **Create Distraction and Confusion**: By creating confusion, chaos, or distractions within the group, you can cause the leader to become overwhelmed, distracted, or ineffective. The more distracted they are, the less control they will have over their followers.
- **Play on Rivalries and Conflicts**: If there are existing rivalries within the group, fan the flames of discord. By creating tensions between the leader and

other influential figures within the group, you can weaken their leadership and sow division among the followers.

- **Isolate the Leader from Their Followers**: Make it difficult for the leader to communicate effectively with their followers. Cut off lines of communication, spread rumors that create mistrust, or even make the leader appear distant or disconnected from the people they are trying to lead.
- **Take Advantage of a Crisis**: During moments of crisis or vulnerability, take swift action to strike at the leader's authority. Use the chaos to introduce alternative solutions or leaders, destabilizing the group and positioning yourself as a viable replacement for the leader.
- **Undermine the Leader's Confidence**: Systematically erode the leader's confidence through criticism, creating doubt about their abilities in both themselves and their followers. Once the leader begins to question their own authority, the followers will begin to question it as well.
- **Appeal to the Followers' Needs and Emotions**: When the leader is weakened or faltering, appeal directly to the followers' emotions or unmet needs. Offer them a solution, vision, or promise that can unite them under a new banner. Once the followers see an alternative, they will scatter from the weakened leader.

Recognizing When Others Use It

- They focus on the primary source of dissent.
- They address influential figures rather than followers.
- They discourage opposition by targeting leaders.
- They avoid engaging with minor players in conflicts.
- They prioritize weakening sources of influence.
- They often shift power dynamics in groups.
- They sidestep low-level resistance, aiming higher.
- They appear unbothered by smaller challenges.
- They focus on the larger picture rather than details.
- They discourage loyalty toward dissenting figures.

How to Neutralize Its Use

- Build a strong, resilient team beyond one leader.
- Avoid centralizing power in a single figure.

- Foster loyalty based on shared goals, not individuals.
- Recognize the importance of collective leadership.
- Encourage open dialogue to reduce dependency.
- Strengthen alliances throughout the group.
- Avoid over-reliance on a single influential figure.
- Address concerns collectively rather than focusing on one.
- Prepare contingency plans for leader transitions.
- Value diversity and independence within the team.

Behaviors that Make You a Target

- **Centralizing Power Around a Single Leader**: If you place too much power in the hands of one person, it becomes easy for others to target and neutralize that person. By centralizing too much influence around a single figure, you set them up as a target and expose their vulnerability.
- **Failing to Build a Broad Support Base**: If the leader fails to cultivate strong, widespread support among their followers, their position is easily threatened. The more isolated and dependent a leader's power base is, the easier it becomes for someone to strike and scatter the group.
- **Ignoring Internal Rivalries or Tensions**: If you neglect or fail to address rivalries and conflicts within your group, you create an environment where these tensions can be exploited. Manipulators will use these internal divisions to destabilize your leadership and cause your followers to scatter.
- **Being Overly Arrogant or Dismissive of Others**: Leaders who are dismissive or arrogant toward their followers create resentment and distance. If followers feel disrespected or overlooked, they are more likely to be swayed by someone who challenges the leader's authority or promises a different vision.
- **Lack of Contingency Plans**: Failing to plan for challenges to your authority, whether from external or internal threats, can leave you vulnerable. Without a plan to deal with potential threats, you become an easy target for those seeking to strike at your leadership.
- **Overextending Yourself**: Leaders who try to take on too many responsibilities or who stretch themselves too thin risk losing control and focus. When a leader is overwhelmed or distracted, their position becomes easier to attack, and their followers may scatter or become disengaged.
- **Underestimating the Power of Influence and Persuasion**: If you are a leader who fails to recognize the power of persuasion and subtle influence,

you leave yourself vulnerable to those who can sway your followers. Those who understand how to manipulate others can easily disrupt your leadership if you don't cultivate loyalty and persuasion skills.

- **Overreliance on One Source of Power**: Relying too heavily on a single source of power (such as wealth, brute force, or charisma) can make you vulnerable if that source is challenged or removed. If your leadership is dependent on just one factor, opponents can easily disrupt your base of power.
- **Not Building Resilience or Loyalty**: Failing to build loyalty and trust among followers means that they can easily be swayed by external forces. Manipulators will exploit a lack of strong relationships to break up the group or remove the leader, knowing that the followers will scatter if the leader's position is shaken.
- **Ignoring the Need for Flexibility**: Rigid, inflexible leadership can invite challenge. If the leader is seen as unwilling to change or adapt, followers may turn to someone more adaptable and dynamic. By being overly dogmatic or resistant to change, you make it easier for others to take advantage of your inability to adjust to new circumstances.

Law—**43**

Work on the Hearts and Minds of Others

"The human heart is the only instrument that can be played by feeling."

— Nathaniel Hawthorne

Law 43: Work on the Hearts and Minds of Others

This law advises winning people over emotionally and intellectually. By appealing to their values and beliefs, you secure their loyalty more effectively than through force or coercion.

The Power Behind the Principle

People are more willing to cooperate when they feel understood and appreciated. Engaging with them on an emotional level fosters genuine loyalty and commitment. The benefit is long-term support and trust.

Putting It to Use

- **Listen Actively and Empathize**: Pay close attention to the emotions, needs, and desires of others. By listening intently and showing genuine empathy, you create a sense of connection and make people feel valued. This will naturally influence them to be more cooperative with your goals.
- **Appeal to People's Self-Interest**: People are more likely to align with you when they see how doing so benefits them. Frame your ideas or requests in ways that highlight the personal advantages or emotional rewards that others will gain from supporting you.
- **Create an Emotional Bond**: People are moved by emotions, so make an effort to form personal connections. Share a bit of vulnerability, show care, and connect on a human level. When people feel emotionally invested in you, they are more likely to follow your lead.
- **Use Flattery (Strategically)**: Compliment others, but do so in a sincere and subtle way. Everyone enjoys being praised for their achievements, intelligence, or qualities. A well-placed compliment can build goodwill and make others more inclined to support you.
- **Appeal to Ideals and Values**: Align yourself with the ideals and values of others. If you know what someone holds dear (whether it's freedom, security, success, or justice), appeal to these values to inspire loyalty and emotional attachment. When you speak to what people care about most, they are more likely to follow you.

- **Make People Feel Important**: People crave recognition and respect. Acknowledge others' contributions and make them feel appreciated. This will make them feel more inclined to cooperate with you and support your vision because they feel seen and valued.
- **Master the Art of Charisma**: Cultivate a magnetic presence. Charisma draws people in and makes them feel special. Use your charm, confidence, and enthusiasm to captivate others and win them over emotionally. Charismatic people are often followed because they make others feel good about themselves.
- **Engage in Persuasive Storytelling**: People are drawn to stories that evoke emotions. Use storytelling as a way to inspire and persuade others. Whether through personal anecdotes or narratives that resonate with the emotions of your audience, a well-crafted story can create an emotional connection and drive action.
- **Be a Source of Inspiration**: Inspire others by embodying the qualities they admire and aspire to. Be passionate about your ideas and vision, and let that passion ignite others. When people feel inspired by you, they are more likely to support your goals and be emotionally invested in your success.
- **Provide a Sense of Belonging**: Make others feel that they are part of something bigger than themselves. People crave community and purpose, so when you offer them a sense of belonging to a cause, a team, or a vision, they are more likely to be emotionally aligned with your mission.

Recognizing When Others Use It

- They express interest in others' values and beliefs.
- They focus on emotional and intellectual connections.
- They avoid force or manipulation in gaining support.
- They build rapport through empathy and understanding.
- They show appreciation for diverse perspectives.
- They are tactful and considerate in discussions.
- They prioritize building genuine relationships.
- They acknowledge others' contributions openly.
- They encourage shared goals and values.
- They create a sense of belonging.

How to Neutralize Its Use

- Engage in open communication to maintain trust.
- Foster mutual understanding and respect.
- Be mindful of emotional influence in interactions.
- Focus on shared goals rather than personal agendas.
- Cultivate a supportive, inclusive environment.
- Acknowledge positive intentions while staying objective.
- Evaluate their motives alongside their actions.
- Build genuine relationships based on transparency.
- Prioritize long-term collaboration over immediate gains.
- Encourage alignment of values within the team.

Behaviors that Make You a Target

- **Being Emotionally Closed Off or Distant**: If you don't allow others to connect with you emotionally or fail to recognize their feelings, you create an emotional distance that can make you susceptible to manipulation. People who can't emotionally relate to you are easier to manipulate, as they are less likely to feel invested in your well-being.
- **Ignoring Others' Needs and Desires**: Focusing solely on your own goals without considering the emotions or self-interests of others will alienate them. Manipulators will easily take advantage of your lack of empathy by offering others what you fail to provide.
- **Failing to Build Trust and Connection**: If you do not work on building relationships or creating emotional bonds with others, they will be more easily swayed by someone who does. Emotional connections create loyalty, and without them, others may be more willing to abandon or betray you.
- **Being Overly Defensive or Closed-Minded**: People who are rigid and defensive often push others away, preventing any emotional connection or understanding. If you are not open to feedback or the opinions of others, manipulators will easily exploit this by playing to others' emotions and needs, while leaving you isolated.
- **Being Too Focused on Logic and Reason**: If you rely solely on logic, reason, and facts to convince people, you may miss the emotional undercurrent that drives their decisions. Neglecting emotional appeal makes you vulnerable to those who can manipulate feelings more effectively.

- **Being Inconsistent or Unpredictable**: If you are unpredictable or inconsistent in your behavior, people will become unsure of where they stand with you. This insecurity can be exploited by manipulators who can prey on others' confusion and uncertainty.
- **Failing to Recognize the Power of Flattery**: If you dismiss compliments and praise without acknowledging them or using them to your advantage, you miss an opportunity to build rapport and emotional attachment. Manipulators often use flattery to influence, and not responding to it appropriately leaves you vulnerable.
- **Neglecting to Inspire or Motivate Others**: If you fail to inspire or motivate people, you leave them without a sense of purpose or drive. People will follow someone who offers them a vision or inspiration, and if you don't provide this, others may be swayed by those who offer a more compelling emotional narrative.
- **Being Dishonest or Insincere**: People can often sense dishonesty, and once they detect that you're insincere or manipulative, they will distance themselves from you. If you come across as fake or deceptive, others will emotionally disconnect, making it easier for more skilled manipulators to take control.
- **Being Overly Focused on Authority and Control**: If you try to control every aspect of a relationship or group through force, intimidation, or authority, you may alienate people emotionally. A strict reliance on control creates resistance and resentment, leaving you vulnerable to those who know how to appeal to people's emotions and create loyalty through empathy and connection.

Law— **44**

Disarm and Infuriate with the Mirror Effect

"Mirror what they admire in you, and you will have them under your control."

— Unknown

Law 44: Disarm and Infuriate with the Mirror Effect

This law suggests reflecting others' behaviors or attitudes back at them to disarm, confuse, or provoke them. By "mirroring" others, you can gain psychological control and often elicit desired reactions.

The Power Behind the Principle

When people see their own behavior mirrored, it can unsettle them, making them more pliable or easier to manipulate. This technique can also foster empathy or defuse conflict by showing others how they appear. The benefit is psychological influence without overt confrontation.

Putting It to Use

- **Imitate the Other's Communication Style**: Pay attention to how someone speaks—whether it's their tone, speed, or specific phrases—and subtly mirror it. This creates rapport and makes them feel more comfortable around you, but also puts them in a position where they may feel like you're mimicking or challenging them.
- **Mirror Their Body Language**: Pay attention to the person's posture, gestures, and facial expressions. By matching their body language subtly (without being too obvious), you can create a bond or make them uncomfortable, depending on your intent. If done correctly, this disarms them and may even create confusion or frustration.
- **Adopt Their Values and Beliefs**: If you want to influence someone, take the time to understand their worldview and adopt similar perspectives, even if they differ from your own. Reflecting their beliefs back to them makes them feel understood and reduces resistance.
- **Copy Their Attitudes or Emotions**: Mirror the emotions that someone is displaying. If they're excited, match their energy. If they're upset, show a similar level of anger or frustration. This emotional mirroring will make them feel seen and heard, but could also unsettle them, especially if they're unaware of what's happening.
- **Mirror Their Decision-Making Process**: If someone is leading with logic, use rational arguments and similar reasoning. If they are more intuitive or

emotional, reflect their approach. By mirroring their decision-making style, you appear more aligned with them, making it easier to influence their thoughts.

- **Reflect Their Weaknesses or Flaws**: If you know the person has insecurities, subtly imitate their behavior or response patterns that highlight these weaknesses. This can make them uncomfortable, but it can also subtly disarm them by causing them to question their own behavior or leadership style.
- **Use Their Own Arguments Against Them**: Take their own reasoning, arguments, or ideas and reflect them back to them, potentially twisting or exaggerating them to expose contradictions. This can disarm your opponent, as they will be forced to confront their own logic or actions.
- **Mirror Their Social Role**: If you want to gain trust or influence within a group, reflect the behaviors or social roles that people in the group admire or aspire to. By showing that you understand the norms and expectations of the group, you disarm opposition and fit in easily.
- **Reflect Their Goals and Desires**: If you can understand the person's deeper desires or motivations, mirror these back in your own words and actions. By aligning yourself with what they want, they'll become more receptive to your influence and less likely to resist your ideas.
- **Respond to Aggression with Calmness**: If someone is aggressive or confrontational, mirror their level of aggression in a calm and controlled manner. This can disarm their attack by reflecting the intensity back to them in a way that confuses them or forces them to back off.

Recognizing When Others Use It

- They mimic your tone, gestures, or expressions.
- They adopt your perspective or repeat your words.
- They seem to mirror your mood or attitude.
- They respond similarly to how you approach situations.
- They replicate your actions in social settings.
- They show empathy by adopting your concerns.
- They avoid direct disagreement, choosing to reflect.
- They subtly imitate your communication style.
- They defuse situations by mirroring your behaviors.
- They appear agreeable without committing fully.

How to Neutralize Its Use

- Recognize mirroring as a potential influence strategy.
- Avoid overreacting to reflected behaviors.
- Stay composed and unaffected by mirrored actions.
- Refocus on your priorities without getting distracted.
- Adjust your approach to prevent continuous mirroring.
- Set boundaries in response to imitation.
- Stay confident in your original stance.
- Avoid allowing their behavior to shape yours.
- Observe if they adapt differently with others.
- Focus on clear goals to prevent manipulation.

Behaviors that Make You a Target

- **Being Predictable in Your Behavior**: If your behavior is easily predictable, others can mirror and manipulate you more effectively. If you always react in the same way to certain stimuli, you're giving others the chance to replicate your actions and influence your responses.
- **Having Strong Emotional Reactions**: If you are highly emotional and reactive, people will more easily mirror your emotions, causing you to become more disoriented or infuriated when you see your own emotional patterns reflected back at you. This can undermine your clarity and cause you to act impulsively.
- **Lacking Self-Awareness**: If you're unaware of your own behaviors or patterns, someone can easily mirror them to gain your trust or unsettle you. Without self-awareness, you may not even realize you're being manipulated by your own reflected actions.
- **Showing Insecurity or Vulnerability**: If you reveal personal insecurities, others can mirror your weakness back to you, which may intensify your sense of insecurity or frustration. This vulnerability can be used against you if your weaknesses are amplified through the mirror effect.
- **Over-Reliance on One Emotional Response**: If you consistently react to stress, conflict, or issues with a specific emotional response (such as anger, frustration, or fear), others can mirror that same response back to you in a way that amplifies your reaction and disrupts your control over the situation.

- **Displaying Inconsistent Behavior**: Inconsistent actions and behaviors make you more vulnerable to manipulation. If you're unpredictable or change your stance frequently, manipulators can mirror your erratic behavior, causing confusion or forcing you into a defensive position.
- **Being Overly Passive or Non-Assertive**: If you are overly passive, defer to others too easily, or avoid confrontation, someone else may reflect this passivity back to you, making you uncomfortable or frustrated when you see your own hesitation mirrored. This can disarm you, leaving you more open to manipulation.
- **Engaging in Public Criticism or Aggression**: If you regularly engage in public criticism, hostility, or aggressive behavior, manipulators may mirror this behavior back to you, causing you to become angry, defensive, or more easily manipulated. It can provoke an emotional response that works against you.
- **Being Too Transparent or Predictable in Your Actions**: If you are too open about your thoughts, plans, or desires, others can mirror your intentions in a way that diverts you from your course or frustrates your progress. People who are too transparent leave themselves vulnerable to manipulation through imitation.
- **Being Emotionally Reactive Instead of Strategic**: When you allow yourself to react emotionally in the heat of the moment rather than taking a strategic approach, others can mirror your emotional reactivity to unsettle you or provoke a stronger emotional response. This plays into their ability to manipulate you emotionally.

Law—**45**

Preach the Need for Change, but Never Reform Too Much at Once

---

"To improve is to change; to be perfect is to change often."

— *Winston Churchill*

Law 45: Preach the Need for Change, but Never Reform Too Much at Once

This law advises making changes gradually rather than overwhelming people with radical reform. By respecting existing values and beliefs, you reduce resistance and maintain stability during transitions.

The Power Behind the Principle

People are often resistant to change, especially when it challenges their established norms. By introducing adjustments incrementally, you reduce opposition and foster acceptance over time. The benefit is smoother transitions and sustained progress.

Putting It to Use

- **Introduce Small, Manageable Changes**: Rather than overhauling everything at once, start with small changes that are easy to implement. These changes will seem less threatening, and over time, they will build momentum for larger shifts.
- **Frame Change as Progress**: When proposing change, position it as a necessary step toward progress and improvement, rather than a complete reinvention. Help others see how each small change will bring them closer to a better future.
- **Focus on Quick Wins**: Prioritize reforms that can yield visible, quick results. This makes people feel like change is already happening, reducing their resistance and increasing their confidence in your ability to lead them through the transformation process.
- **Involve Others in the Change Process**: Rather than imposing change from the top down, get buy-in by involving people in the process. Ask for feedback, input, and participation, allowing them to feel they have a role in shaping the changes, which reduces the feeling of being "forced" into something new.
- **Communicate the Benefits of Change Clearly**: Explain the reasons for the change and how it will benefit those involved. By focusing on the positive outcomes, you can overcome skepticism and foster a sense of excitement about the future.

- **Use Incremental Steps to Build Consensus**: Break larger goals into smaller, easier-to-digest steps. This approach makes people feel less overwhelmed by the idea of change and allows you to build consensus slowly, gaining support as you go.
- **Create a Sense of Urgency Without Panic**: While you should emphasize the need for change, avoid creating panic. Inspire action with a sense of urgency, but reassure others that the change will happen gradually and with their well-being in mind.
- **Implement Change in Phases**: Roll out your changes in phases, giving people time to adjust to each phase before moving to the next. This allows them to become comfortable with one change before another is introduced, reducing fear and resistance.
- **Leverage Success Stories from Similar Changes**: Share examples of how gradual change has been successful in other contexts, whether within the organization, industry, or even personal anecdotes. This shows others that the path you are suggesting is tried, tested, and has worked for others.
- **Prepare for Resistance and Address Concerns**: Anticipate that not everyone will welcome the change immediately. Prepare for resistance and offer reassurance, addressing concerns with patience and understanding. This makes the change feel less threatening and more manageable.

Recognizing When Others Use It

- They introduce new ideas gradually.
- They avoid making drastic changes all at once.
- They frame changes as natural progress.
- They respect established norms while innovating.
- They emphasize continuity despite changes.
- They focus on incremental improvements.
- They are patient with resistance to change.
- They adapt their reforms to existing systems.
- They use familiar language to introduce new ideas.
- They gradually build support for their initiatives.

How to Neutralize Its Use

- Recognize incremental change as intentional strategy.
- Stay alert to long-term shifts despite subtle changes.
- Observe any cumulative impacts of small reforms.
- Question the purpose behind gradual changes.
- Assess each change individually for alignment.
- Avoid complacency in response to incrementalism.
- Seek clarification on the larger vision behind reforms.
- Be cautious of subtle shifts in expectations.
- Maintain awareness of your values amid gradual change.
- Engage in open dialogue to understand intentions.

Behaviors that Make You a Target

- **Pushing for Radical, Abrupt Change**: If you push for sweeping, immediate changes without considering the existing systems or the comfort levels of others, it will provoke resistance. People need time to adjust, and when you push too hard or too fast, you risk alienating your audience.
- **Overlooking the Need for Gradual Transition**: If you attempt to reform everything at once, you will overwhelm those around you. Change that is too sudden or too broad can cause anxiety, confusion, and rejection, making people resistant to the ideas you are trying to implement.
- **Ignoring the Emotional Impact of Change**: Change is not just a rational process; it's emotional as well. If you fail to consider how people will feel about the changes you are proposing, you risk creating unnecessary resistance or hostility. Ignoring these emotional aspects makes it easier for others to manipulate you or derail your plans.
- **Being Overly Dogmatic About Change**: If you are rigid and uncompromising in your desire for change, it will backfire. People resist those who seem inflexible and unwilling to accommodate their concerns. Being too aggressive in pushing change makes it easier for others to manipulate you by exploiting your lack of adaptability.
- **Failing to Gain Consensus**: If you implement change without consulting others or gaining their support, you risk creating discontent and alienation. When people feel excluded from the decision-making process, they may manipulate you by undermining your efforts or creating friction.

- **Underestimating People's Fear of Change**: People fear uncertainty, and if you overlook this psychological aspect, they will react with resistance, sabotage, or passive-aggression. If you don't address their fears and help them feel comfortable with the changes, they may begin to actively work against you.

- **Overloading People with Information**: When introducing change, bombarding people with excessive amounts of information too quickly can overwhelm them and make them retreat into resistance. If they feel like they are being forced to learn or adapt too quickly, it can cause frustration and confusion.

- **Failing to Highlight Quick Wins and Early Successes**: If you do not take the time to celebrate and highlight small successes as part of the change process, you risk creating the perception that the change is failing. This opens the door for manipulators to exploit this perception and derail your efforts.

- **Disregarding the Current System's Strengths**: If you fail to acknowledge the existing systems or processes that are already working, people may feel like you're dismantling something that is valuable. This can create resentment and make people less likely to support future changes.

- **Not Having a Clear Vision or Plan**: If your vision for change is unclear or lacks a well-structured plan, people will feel uncertain about the direction you're leading them in. This uncertainty makes it easier for others to manipulate you by sowing doubt or confusion about the proposed changes.

Part X

Your Path to Power

Law 46: Never Appear to Perfect
Use relatability to win trust and diffuse envy.

Law 47: Do Not Go Past the Mark You Aimed For; In Victory, Learn When to Stop
Recognize the limits of success to avoid self-destruction.

Law 48: Assume Formlessness
Flexibility is the ultimate form of strength and resilience.

Law — **46**

Never Appear Too Perfect

"The imperfections of a diamond shine more than a flawless pearl."

— Kahlil Gibran

Law 46: Never Appear Too Perfect

This law suggests showing some flaws or vulnerabilities to avoid envy and resentment from others. By appearing human rather than perfect, you inspire empathy and reduce potential antagonism.

The Power Behind the Principle

Excessive perfection can provoke jealousy and create distance. Showing a few weaknesses makes you relatable, fostering better relationships and reducing rivalry. The benefit is gaining loyalty and support without stirring resentment.

Putting It to Use

- **Show Vulnerability**: Occasionally share personal challenges, struggles, or flaws. This allows others to connect with you on a deeper level, humanizing you and making you more relatable. People are more likely to trust and support someone who shows authenticity and imperfection.
- **Highlight Your Mistakes**: Don't shy away from admitting when you've made a mistake. Acknowledging your errors helps to build credibility, as people appreciate honesty and transparency. It also prevents others from thinking you're hiding something or are too good to be true.
- **Avoid Bragging About Your Achievements**: If you constantly boast about your successes, you may come off as arrogant or self-centered. Instead, allow your achievements to speak for themselves and remain modest about your accomplishments.
- **Embrace Criticism**: Be open to feedback and criticism. Rather than defending yourself or trying to justify everything, take the opportunity to learn and improve. This shows that you are humble and grounded, which makes others more comfortable around you.
- **Let Others See You Struggle**: While you should strive for excellence, it's important to let others see that achieving success often requires hard work, setbacks, and failure. This makes you appear more human and helps others relate to your journey.
- **Engage in Small, Imperfect Acts**: Do things that show you are not afraid to look imperfect. For instance, participate in activities where you're not an

expert, and let others see that you're willing to learn and grow from your mistakes.

- **Acknowledge Your Flaws Publicly**: If appropriate, acknowledge your weaknesses or limitations in a public or professional setting. Whether it's admitting you struggle with a particular skill or that you are working to improve an aspect of your personality, this builds trust and makes you seem more authentic.
- **Show Humility in Leadership**: As a leader, avoid presenting yourself as an infallible figure. Share the credit for successes with your team, and acknowledge that you depend on others for your achievements. Humility makes you appear more grounded and approachable.
- **Use Humor to Disarm Perfectionism**: Use self-deprecating humor to show that you don't take yourself too seriously. By making fun of your own imperfections, you signal that you're human and that you understand the importance of laughter and perspective.
- **Balance Confidence with Humility**: While it's important to be confident, make sure your confidence is balanced with humility. Don't let your self-assurance come across as arrogance. By showing that you are secure in your abilities but also open to improvement, you prevent others from feeling threatened.

Recognizing When Others Use It

- They reveal minor flaws or mistakes.
- They avoid appearing overly confident or flawless.
- They downplay achievements modestly.
- They acknowledge challenges or struggles.
- They are open to constructive criticism.
- They avoid making others feel inferior.
- They focus on collaboration rather than competition.
- They highlight teamwork over personal success.
- They express gratitude and humility.
- They share credit with others.

How to Neutralize Its Use

- Recognize the potential for hidden strengths.

- Avoid underestimating their abilities.
- Respect their modesty but stay mindful of their influence.
- Appreciate their transparency without overemphasizing it.
- Focus on the team's achievements collectively.
- Maintain a balanced view of their capabilities.
- Acknowledge your own contributions confidently.
- Avoid overly critical assessments of their flaws.
- Build mutual respect through genuine interactions.
- Embrace the value of both strengths and vulnerabilities.

Behaviors that Make You a Target

- **Constantly Striving for Perfection**: If you constantly try to present yourself as flawless or perfect, others will view you as unattainable or arrogant. This creates envy, which can lead to manipulation as people may try to bring you down to their level or sabotage your success.
- **Being Unwilling to Admit Weaknesses**: If you refuse to acknowledge any shortcomings or flaws, you appear inhuman or overly self-assured. This can make others feel disconnected from you and may prompt them to manipulate you to expose your vulnerabilities.
- **Bragging About Success**: Constantly highlighting your achievements without any acknowledgment of effort or failure can create jealousy and resentment. People may attempt to manipulate you by undermining your achievements or playing on your insecurities.
- **Exaggerating Your Achievements**: If you inflate your successes or pretend to be more capable than you actually are, others will eventually see through it. This leads to a lack of trust, making it easier for others to manipulate or discredit you.
- **Being Overly Critical of Others**: If you are overly critical or dismissive of others' mistakes or shortcomings, you will make them feel inferior and disconnected. In turn, this may lead them to try and bring you down or manipulate you by exploiting your need for perfection.
- **Avoiding Failure at All Costs**: If you present yourself as someone who never fails, you invite resentment from those who may see you as dishonest or pretending to be invincible. People may begin to manipulate you by creating situations where your perfection is exposed as a facade.

- **Not Showing Vulnerability or Emotions**: People who never show their emotions or vulnerabilities can seem distant or unapproachable. This can lead to manipulation because others may try to find a way to force you to show weakness or to use your lack of emotional transparency against you.
- **Trying to Control Everything**: If you try to maintain perfect control over every situation and every outcome, others may feel stifled or resentful. This can lead to manipulation as they work to undermine your authority or make you appear incompetent.
- **Being Overly Competitive**: If you always try to outdo others and present yourself as the best, you create an environment of rivalry and resentment. This opens the door for manipulation, as people may attempt to use your need to win as a way to control or influence your actions.
- **Refusing to Accept Help or Support**: If you always insist on doing everything on your own, refusing to accept help from others, it makes you seem like you believe you are above others. This can isolate you, creating a perception of arrogance or superiority, which can be used against you in manipulative ways.

Law — **47**

Do Not Go Past the Mark You Aimed For; In Victory, Learn When to Stop

---

"Know when to hold 'em, know when to fold 'em."

— Kenny Rogers

Law 47: Do Not Go Past the Mark You Aimed For; In Victory, Learn When to Stop

This law advises knowing when to cease further efforts after a victory, as overreaching can turn success into failure. By stopping at the right moment, you avoid creating unnecessary risks or provoking others.

The Power Behind the Principle

Success can lead to overconfidence, causing people to push beyond their original goals. Learning when to stop solidifies your achievements and prevents potential backlash. The benefit is sustained success and a strong reputation without diminishing returns.

Putting It to Use

- **Set Clear, Specific Goals**: Start by establishing clear and achievable goals. This will give you a precise target and allow you to recognize when you have accomplished what you set out to do, preventing you from overextending yourself.
- **Assess the Situation Regularly**: Keep a close eye on the progress of your goal and assess whether the conditions have changed. This will help you gauge when you've achieved what you aimed for and when to stop before you push too far.
- **Take Time to Reflect on Your Success**: After achieving your objective, pause and reflect on what you've accomplished. Celebrate the victory and understand that going any further might spoil the positive outcomes or create unnecessary complications.
- **Avoid Greed or Overreach**: Resist the temptation to push beyond your original goal, especially if it involves gaining more power, resources, or influence. Overreaching can lead to opposition and ultimately diminish your initial success.
- **Pay Attention to Feedback**: Listen to the reactions and feedback from others. If people are becoming uneasy or resistant to further advances, take it as a signal that you have reached your limit and should stop.

- **Understand the Law of Diminishing Returns**: Recognize that the more you push beyond your goal, the less you are likely to gain. The benefits of continued effort may decrease as you stretch yourself too thin, and the risk of damaging your success increases.
- **Know When to Exit**: Just as in a negotiation or a deal, understand when you've gained enough. Exiting at the right moment can maximize your victory and ensure that you leave on top without risking future losses.
- **Maintain Control Over Emotions**: Avoid letting emotions like greed, pride, or overconfidence cloud your judgment. It is important to remain rational and objective, recognizing that sometimes stopping is the best choice to protect your position.
- **Reinforce Your Achievements**: After achieving your goal, take the time to solidify your position by building lasting relationships and alliances that support your success. This helps you maintain your victory without pushing for more.
- **Communicate the End Point**: Be clear about your goals with others. If people understand that you have a clear end point, they will respect the boundaries and not attempt to push you past the mark you aimed for.

Recognizing When Others Use It

- They achieve a goal and then refrain from further action.
- They celebrate success modestly without overextending.
- They remain focused on the original objectives.
- They avoid showing excessive ambition after victory.
- They express gratitude and humility in success.
- They focus on stability rather than further gains.
- They emphasize sustained growth over rapid expansion.
- They set boundaries on their achievements.
- They reinforce existing accomplishments.
- They avoid creating competition with new actions.

How to Neutralize Its Use

- Recognize the importance of knowing your limits.
- Avoid pushing for excessive gains after initial success.
- Focus on securing what has already been achieved.

- Celebrate accomplishments without overreaching.
- Maintain realistic expectations after victory.
- Plan for stability rather than endless growth.
- Avoid being provoked into further challenges.
- Appreciate the balance between ambition and caution.
- Encourage team celebration without additional demands.
- Respectfully reinforce their boundaries after success.

Behaviors that Make You a Target

- **Pushing for More After a Victory**: If you keep pushing for more after achieving your initial goal, others may start to see you as greedy or excessively ambitious. This can provoke resistance, and others may manipulate your desire for more to control your actions or undermine your success.
- **Ignoring the Signs of Overreach**: Not paying attention to signals that you've gone too far—such as resistance from allies or growing resentment from others—can lead to your downfall. If you keep pushing when it's no longer necessary, you become vulnerable to being manipulated by those who want to bring you down.
- **Refusing to Acknowledge When Enough is Enough**: If you refuse to acknowledge when you've gained all that you need and continue to demand more, you risk alienating people. Manipulators will exploit your inability to recognize when to stop, using it to create chaos or turn others against you.
- **Prideful Overconfidence**: If you let your success go to your head and start overestimating your position, you risk pushing too far. People will take advantage of your overconfidence, pushing you into situations where you will overreach and lose everything.
- **Taking Victory for Granted**: If you assume that your victory is permanent and don't take steps to consolidate it, you risk losing it all. Others may manipulate you by exploiting your complacency, knowing that you haven't taken the necessary precautions to protect your success.
- **Becoming Complacent in Success**: If you rest too long on your laurels, failing to adapt or innovate after success, your position may erode. This makes you vulnerable to being manipulated by those who are more dynamic and alert to opportunities.

- **Failing to Consider the Bigger Picture**: Over-focus on your current victory without considering the broader implications or long-term consequences can lead to mistakes. You may be manipulated by those who understand the bigger picture and can use your narrow vision against you.
- **Pushing Allies Too Hard**: If you push your allies or supporters to go beyond what they are comfortable with in pursuit of more power or success, you will lose their support. Manipulators may exploit your strained relationships to cause division and take advantage of your weakened position.
- **Ignoring the Limits of Power**: If you continue to expand your power without recognizing natural limits or boundaries, you risk alienating those around you. Others may exploit your overextension to create obstacles that force you to scale back.
- **Not Knowing When to Walk Away**: If you lack the ability to walk away from a successful situation or to stop when you're ahead, you open yourself up to manipulation. Manipulators will use your inability to stop to push you into situations that will endanger your position or success.

Law — **48**

Assume Formlessness

"The wise adapt themselves to circumstances, as water molds itself to the pitcher."

— *Chinese Proverb*

Law 48: Assume Formlessness

This law advises remaining adaptable and avoiding rigid forms or predictable patterns. By staying flexible, you make yourself harder to control, anticipate, or oppose. Formlessness allows you to flow with change and adapt to any situation.

The Power Behind the Principle

Rigidity can lead to vulnerability, as predictable behavior makes you an easy target. By remaining fluid and formless, you're able to respond to change, evade traps, and outmaneuver those who seek to control you. The benefit is resilience and the ability to navigate a wide range of circumstances.

Putting It to Use

- **Embrace Flexibility in Your Strategy**: Rather than sticking rigidly to one plan, be ready to adapt your approach depending on circumstances. Constantly assess the situation and change your tactics to meet new challenges, which keeps others off-balance and unable to anticipate your next move.
- **Stay Unpredictable**: Avoid being predictable in your actions, whether in your career, relationships, or business. By changing your behavior or approach unexpectedly, you prevent others from gaining leverage over you, forcing them to remain on edge.
- **Blend In**: Don't call attention to yourself unnecessarily. Whether in a group setting or a leadership role, avoid drawing too much attention to your actions or opinions. Blend in with others to avoid being singled out or targeted.
- **Create Multiple Personas**: Adapt your behavior to suit different situations and individuals. By assuming different roles, you can navigate various environments without being pinned down to one persona. This versatility makes it harder for others to control you or anticipate your next move.
- **Stay Fluid in Your Relationships**: Avoid locking yourself into permanent alliances or enmities. Keep your relationships flexible, and be willing to shift your alliances as the situation changes. This makes you less vulnerable to manipulation by any one person or group.

- **Avoid Setting Fixed Goals**: Rather than setting rigid goals that limit your options, keep your objectives flexible and open-ended. This allows you to move in any direction that suits the current situation and prevents others from trapping you into a specific course of action.
- **Keep Your Plans Private**: Don't share all of your intentions with others, and avoid making commitments that bind you to a particular outcome. By maintaining a level of secrecy and ambiguity around your plans, you prevent others from predicting or controlling your moves.
- **Use Deception and Misdirection**: By creating false impressions or misleading signals, you can confuse others about your true intentions. This formlessness allows you to manipulate perceptions and keep others guessing about your next move, thereby gaining the upper hand.
- **Change Your Approach When Under Pressure**: When faced with opposition or obstacles, change your approach rather than becoming entrenched in your current strategy. This adaptability will disarm those trying to predict your actions or trap you into a certain path.
- **Be Patient and Wait for the Right Moment**: For formlessness to be effective, you must exercise patience. Let the environment shift around you and wait for the right opportunity to act. By doing so, you avoid making hasty decisions and are able to adapt more effectively when the time is right.

Recognizing When Others Use It

- They avoid routine or repetitive behaviors.
- They adapt quickly to changing circumstances.
- They avoid declaring long-term plans or rigid stances.
- They remain open to new ideas or perspectives.
- They demonstrate a willingness to reinvent themselves.
- They keep others uncertain about their next move.
- They are comfortable with ambiguity.
- They often act unpredictably, keeping others off balance.
- They avoid labels, roles, or titles that limit them.
- They seem equally at ease in varied situations.

How to Neutralize Its Use

- Avoid making assumptions about their intentions.

- Stay adaptable and avoid rigid expectations.
- Be prepared for multiple potential outcomes.
- Focus on your own goals without trying to control them.
- Cultivate flexibility in your own actions.
- Remain steady despite their unpredictability.
- Avoid depending on their consistency.
- Observe patterns in their adaptability.
- Seek clarity when ambiguity arises.
- Use your own adaptability to counter theirs.

Behaviors that Make You a Target

- **Being Too Rigid in Your Plans or Actions**: If you cling to a fixed strategy or set of beliefs, others will be able to predict your behavior and use that to manipulate you. Being inflexible makes you a target, as people can exploit your predictability and use it against you.
- **Revealing Your Full Intentions**: When you openly share all your goals and plans, others can anticipate your moves and use your own information to undermine you. Keeping your intentions vague or hidden prevents others from taking advantage of you.
- **Always Sticking to One Role or Persona**: If you consistently behave in the same way or play the same role in every situation, people will come to understand your behavior patterns. This predictability can be exploited, as others can anticipate your responses and manipulate your actions.
- **Being Transparent About Your Weaknesses**: If you openly discuss your vulnerabilities or weaknesses, you give others the power to exploit them. By remaining elusive and not revealing too much about yourself, you make it harder for others to take advantage of your flaws.
- **Overcommitting to One Group or Cause**: If you pledge your loyalty too openly to a single group, cause, or individual, you make yourself a predictable ally and an easier target for manipulation. Formlessness requires that you maintain flexibility in your alliances and remain ready to switch sides when necessary.
- **Over-explaining Your Actions or Intentions**: When you feel the need to constantly justify your actions or decisions, you give others the chance to analyze and manipulate your motivations. Keeping your actions vague and mysterious keeps others uncertain about your true objectives.

- **Being Overconfident in Your Ability to Control a Situation**: If you believe that you have absolute control or certainty about the outcome of a situation, you become rigid and inflexible. This opens you up to manipulation, as others can exploit your overconfidence and use your assumptions against you.
- **Letting Your Guard Down**: If you become too comfortable or complacent in your position, you may stop adapting and become an easy target for manipulation. Remaining fluid and vigilant prevents others from gaining the upper hand by exploiting your moment of relaxation.
- **Being Too Loyal or Committed to One Person**: If you put all your trust in one person, that person can use your loyalty to manipulate you. A key part of formlessness is not allowing yourself to be tethered to one individual or group for too long, making it harder for others to exploit you through emotional or professional manipulation.
- **Clinging to a Past Identity or Reputation**: If you allow yourself to be defined by past successes, failures, or identities, you limit your ability to change and grow. Others can use this fixed perception to manipulate you or make you feel trapped in your former self. Stay fluid and adaptable to avoid being controlled by your past.

Closing Chapter: Your Journey to Power

As we reach the final chapter of this book, I hope you've discovered more than just the tools and strategies for navigating the complexities of power. I hope you've found encouragement, clarity, and inspiration to define power on your own terms. Because if there's one truth about power, it's this: it isn't something you're given; it's something you claim, something you embody, something you live.

This journey has been about more than just mastering the 48 Laws of Power. It's been about stepping into your confidence, breaking through barriers, and empowering yourself to lead with purpose and authenticity. Now, as you turn the final page, let's reflect on where you've been, where you are, and where you're going.

Your Journey to Power

Power begins with knowing who you are and what you stand for. It's about understanding the dynamics around you and using them to your advantage—not as manipulation but as a way to stand firm in your truth.

Over the chapters, we've explored strategies for:

- **Building your foundation:** Learning how to protect your reputation, adapt to challenges, and plan with intention.
- **Owning your influence:** Using your voice, your presence, and your actions to shape the world around you.
- **Navigating relationships:** Understanding people's motivations, managing conflict, and creating mutually beneficial alliances.
- **Sustaining power:** Balancing strength with adaptability, confidence with humility, and boldness with wisdom.

Every step has been a reminder that power is a skill, not a fixed trait. It can be learned, refined, and used to create the life and legacy you deserve.

Redefining Power on Your Terms

For generations, power has been defined in narrow, often rigid terms—domination, control, and aggression. But as women, we have the opportunity to reshape that narrative. Power doesn't have to mean stepping on others to rise; it can mean lifting others up while you climb. It doesn't have to mean silencing your heart to appear strong; it can mean embracing your empathy as a source of strength.

Redefining power starts with these truths:

Power is collaborative, not competitive: True influence comes from connection, not control. By building networks and supporting others, you create a foundation for mutual growth.

Power is purposeful, not aimless: Power without direction is hollow. Define what success means to you and align your strategies with your purpose.

Power is personal, not performative: Authenticity is your greatest strength. Own your individuality and use it to shape how you lead.

Building Your Legacy

What do you want your legacy to be? For some, it might be blazing a trail in their career. For others, it could be creating a community, mentoring future leaders, or simply living a life that inspires others to do the same. Whatever your vision, remember that power isn't just about the present—it's about the impact you leave behind.

Ask yourself, who do I want to empower along the way? What values will guide my decisions? How will I ensure my success benefits more than just myself? Your legacy is being written every day through your actions, your choices, and the way you treat others. Make it a story worth telling.

Next Steps for Empowerment

Here are some practical steps to keep building on what you've learned:

- Set Long-Term Goals: Define clear, measurable objectives for where you want to be in one year, five years, or ten years. Break them into actionable steps.
- Surround Yourself with Support: Build a network of mentors, allies, and collaborators who inspire and challenge you.
- Invest in Your Growth: Keep learning—whether it's through books, courses, or experiences—and stay curious about the world around you.
- Embrace Challenges: Don't fear setbacks. Use them as opportunities to reflect, adjust, and come back stronger.
- Practice the Laws: Return to the strategies in this book whenever you face uncertainty. They are tools, not rules—adapt them to fit your needs.

Closing Thoughts: The Power Is Yours

As women, we face unique challenges in navigating the landscapes of leadership, influence, and success. But with those challenges come unique strengths—our resilience, our empathy, our ability to adapt. This book has been about equipping you with strategies, but more importantly, it's been about reminding you of the power you already possess.

As you step forward, know that you don't have to do everything at once. Start small. Test the waters. Grow into your power day by day. And remember: you are not alone in this journey. Every step you take toward owning your power is a step that inspires others to do the same.

You are capable. You are powerful. And you are enough.

Now, go claim your power—and use it to create the life you've always deserved!

All Reviews Are Welcomed and Appreciated!

If you found this book to be helpful and would like to help make other women aware of it, please leave us a review wherever you purchased from.

Thank You!

Follow Mary at:

www. maryrobbins.ceo